Herrings, Drifters and the Prunier Trop

Aspects of the vanished herring fishing industry at Great Yarmouth, Lowestoft and Southwold

By
Malcolm R. White

The Sea and Land Heritage Research Series
2006

GENERAL INFORMATION

Published by	Malcolm R. White	Printed by	Micropress Printers Ltd.
	Coastal Publications		27 Norwich Road
	71 Beeching Drive		Halesworth
	Lowestoft		Suffolk
	NR32 4TB		IP19 8BX
	First Published June 2006		ISBN 09547323 4 0
	Copyright © Malcolm R. White 2006		All rights reserved

Every effort has been made to ensure the information contained in this publication is accurate and for this reason numerous sources of information have been consulted. These include personal accounts of events, official documentation, local diaries, media resources and numerous accredited research works. However, when considering such a complex, varied and historical subject with some details gathered from hand written records that were provided by other parties and are often difficult to read, 100% accuracy cannot be guaranteed. By popular request, all measurements, dimensions and distances in this heritage book are stated in British Imperial, not the European metric system. Books in this series are part of the National Published Archive and as such are included in the library collections of the British Library, the National Library of Scotland, the National Library of Wales, the Universities of Oxford and Cambridge, Trinity College, Dublin and, when appropriate, The National Museum of Science & Industry. Unlike the great majority of similar works, this book is not produced for commercial gain for the author or publisher, profits from the series are donated to charities and good causes.

OTHER TITLES IN THIS HERITAGE SERIES

DOWN THE HARBOUR 1955-1995	40 years of fishing vessels, owners, the harbour and shipyards at Lowestoft	ISBN 09532485 0X
A CENTURY OF FISHING	Fishing from Great Yarmouth and Lowestoft 1899-1999	ISBN 09532485 18
FISHING WITH DIVERSITY	A portrait of the Colne Group of Lowestoft	ISBN 09532485 26
CROWNIES OF LOWESTOFT	The steam trawler fleet of Consolidated Fisheries	ISBN 09532485 34
DRIFTING, TRAWLING & SHIPPING	A portrait of Small & Co. (Lowestoft) Ltd.	ISBN 09532485 42
GREETINGS FROM LOWESTOFT	A picture book of old postcards and photographs	ISBN 09532485 50
THE LOWESTOFT TRAIN	The railway at Lowestoft and scenes on the lines to Norwich, Ipswich and Yarmouth	ISBN 09532485 69
LOWESTOFT ANTIQUITY	A picture book of once familiar scenes	ISBN 09532485 77
THE BOSTON PUTFORD STORY (1)	Fishing and Offshore Support from Great Yarmouth and Lowestoft	ISBN 09532485 85
LOWESTOFT CORPORATION TRANSPORT	Lowestoft Trams, Buses and Bygone Town Scenes	ISBN 09532485 93
RAILS TO THE COAST	East Anglian Seaside Stations, Sheds and Rail Links-Great Yarmouth and Lowestoft	ISBN 09547323 08
THE YARMOUTH TRAIN	The railway at Gt. Yarmouth and scenes on the lines to Norwich, Ipswich, Melton Constable and Lowestoft	ISBN 09547323 24
A SMILE FROM OLD LOWESTOFT	A celebration of bygone scenes, achievements and features	ISBN 09847323 32

PHOTOGRAPHS

Front Cover (Top) The Scottish drifter PD593 *Foxglove,* was built in 1918 at the Fraserburgh shipyard of J. & G. Forbes as the standard drifter HMD *Firmament.* She is seen here at the Yarmouth harbour entrance in October 1938. *(MWC)* **Front Cover** (Bottom) An early 1930s colour print showing a group of Scotch girls apparently top tiering barrels of herring ready for sealing and finally topping up with brine. (*LESMS*) **Title page** -With the Herring Industry Board flags indicating drifters can proceed to sea, but may only use eight nets per crew member, LT1147 *Young Mun*, LT63 *Sussex County,* LT47 *Peace Wave* and other drifters leave the harbour at Lowestoft for the fishing grounds in the 1930s. *(MWC)* **Opposite Page** -The crew of YH126 *Young Cliff* clean and check the nets at Yarmouth in the late 1950s. Built in 1925 at the Lowestoft shipyard of John Chambers, the *Young Cliff* was owned by Charles H. Eastick. Originally the *Plankton*, her fishing registry closed on 12th March 1960, the drifter having been broken up. (*MWC*)

CONTENTS

ACKNOWLEDGEMENTS

Much appreciated has been the cooperation and support offered during the preparation of this book by a number of kind people interested in researching and recording the local fishing heritage. These include in particular, Mr. Peter Killby, well known for his knowledge of local history and fishing vessels, and Mr. Stuart Jones BA, who has provided editorial support for all the many titles in this popular series. Assisting either directly or indirectly in this complex project have been Mr. Peter Calvert, Mr. George Catchpole, Mr. Stanley Earl, the late Mr. Ernest Harvey, the late Mr. Ken Kent, Mr. David Moyse, Mrs. Myrtle Parker and Mr. Peter Parker, Mr. Terry Reeve, Mr. Parry Watson, Mr. John Wells and Mr. David White. Valuable information has been provided from the Port of Lowestoft Research Society records and the Society newsletter, the current Editor of which is Mr. Alan Page, the Chairman of the Society. For specific commercial, maritime and fisheries information the following sources have been consulted :- Gulf of Maine Research Institute, Portland, Maine, USA; Various Lloyds Registers of Ships, Various Olsens Fisherman Nautical Almanacks, Ministry of Foreign Affairs, Norway; Norges Sildesalgslag, Bergen, Norway; The Food and Agriculture Organisation of the United Nations (Fisheries); Tyne and Wear Museums; Shetland Museums Services; Eurofish International; Wikimedia; Fisheries Research Services, Aberdeen; Marine Research Institute, Iceland and the Sea Fish Industry Authority.

PHOTOGRAPHIC OWNERSHIP AND COPYRIGHT

Completed as HMD *Grey Sea* in 1918 by J. W. Brooke at Oulton Broad, YH78 *Rosebay* was always a smart looking vessel. A much travelled standard drifter, she had a number of identities before coming into local ownership in the early 1950s. (*DW*)

INTRODUCTION

Being an island people, fishing has always been a natural occupation, and in East Anglia with its close association with the sea, the famous autumn herring fishery, known locally as the "home fishing", proved to be one of the most ancient and staple occupations. After years of decline, the fishery which had principally been centred upon Great Yarmouth and Lowestoft, finally ended in the late 1960s. South of Lowestoft, the port of Southwold was also involved but to a much lesser extent. It should be emphasised that the East Anglian autumn herring fishery was to a large extent Scottish led, both in the land based workforce, the participating vessels and the crews. At one time hundreds of drifters, the fishing vessels used to catch the herring, could be seen at all three ports and the amazing sight of large numbers of these vessels, the great majority being Scottish, setting sail to seek the shoals of herring will never again be witnessed. Fortunately, extensive photographic records exist recalling the "home fishing". As the years pass, fewer people who were actively involved in the fishery, or witnessed what the herring fishing meant to Great Yarmouth and Lowestoft remain. Indeed in the 21st century, how many residents know what a drifter was, eat herrings today, or know how to prepare them ready for the table? The East Anglia herring season generally ran from early October until late November, when the local drifters were joined by hundreds of others from Scotland and a few from elsewhere. As many as 400 million herring have been landed in one season, and exceptionally, 60 million in a single day at the two ports. The 'Yarmouth bloater' was one feature of this industry, and another, the advent of the Scotch fisher girls, for whom Yarmouth, Lowestoft or Southwold was the terminus of their annual migration. Whilst hundreds of these ladies travelled direct by the railway to the three towns, others followed the herring drifters down the east coast, gutting and packing the fish at ports such as Whitby, Scarborough, North Shields and Grimsby when the drifters landed their catches there. Eventually in the autumn, they arrived in East Anglia.
The total collapse of the fishery in the 1960s brought about by the non-appearance of the herrings on the traditional fishing grounds had a major effect on the local economies of both Great Yarmouth and Lowestoft, with fishing companies and their workforces being badly affected, and many long standing trades and suppliers associated with the fishing industry losing trade and closing down.

This book has been published in 2006 to mark the 40th anniversary of the final competition for the Prunier Herring Trophy.

Malcolm White
June 2006

Past Reflections
(MWC)

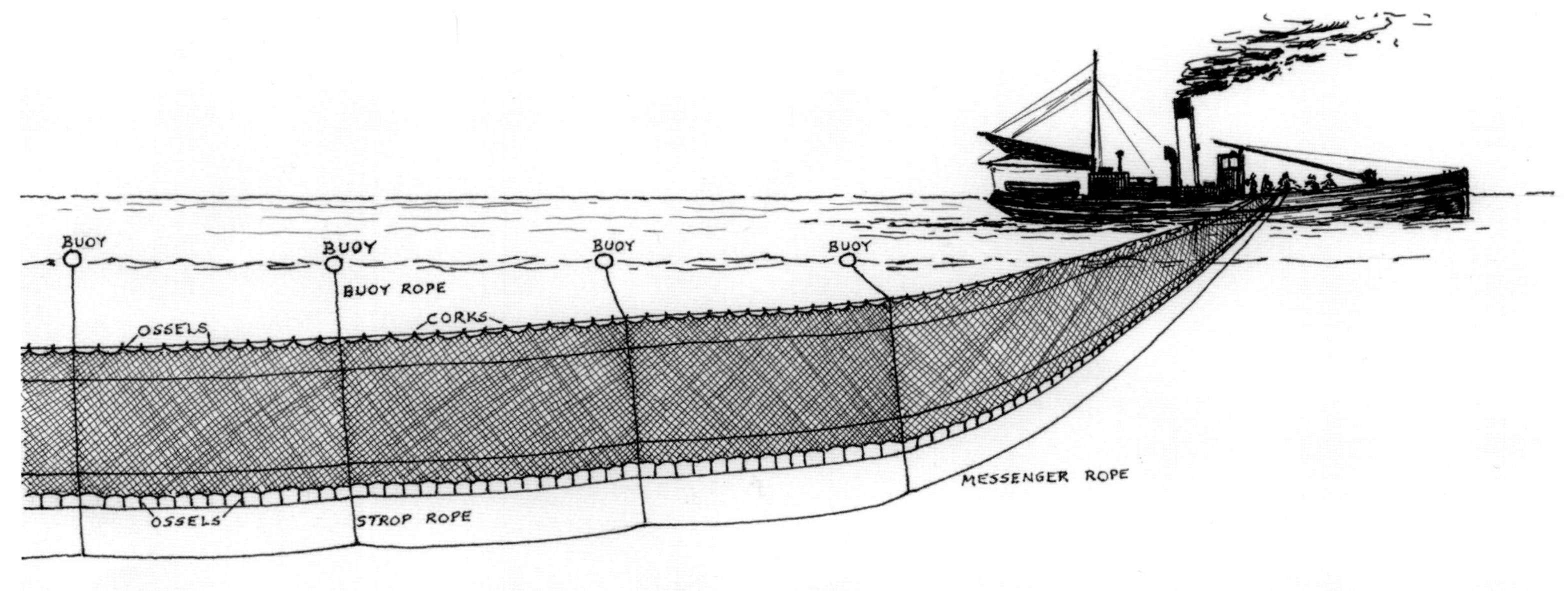

DRIFTER SHOOTING NETS

ELLIOTT & GARROOD LTD. No.3599(1)

HERRING DRIFT NET FISHING-Depending upon the locality, the terms used in these diagrams may differ e.g.

Messenger Rope-Warp-Leader-Buss *Guy Rope*-Tissot *Buoy*-Buff *Buoy Rope*-Strop *Strop Rope*-Seizing

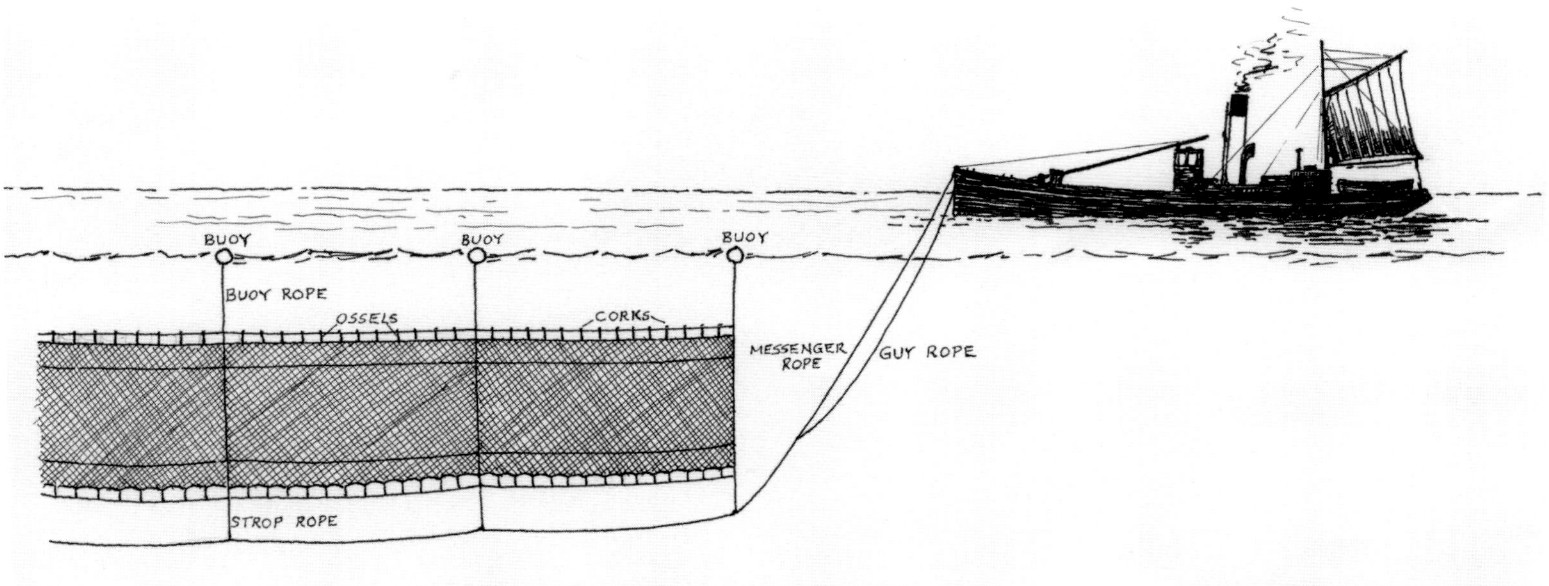

DRIFTER WITH FISHING GEAR DOWN

ELLIOTT & GARROOD LTD. No. 3599(2)

Herrings and Drift Net Fishing

Herring
The silvery streamlined fish associated with the one time East Anglian autumn fishing season and commonly known as the herring (*Clupea harengus*), is one of almost 200 herring species in the family Clupeidae found worldwide.

HERRING
(*Clupea harengus*) *Length from 8 to 15 inches*

Herring survive by feeding on plankton, tiny microscopic organisms that drift freely with the oceanic currents. There are two basic types of plankton: phytoplankton (plants) and zooplankton (animals). The zooplankton community comprises of invertebrate and fish larvae as well as many species that remain drifters for life (holoplankton). This is thought by some scientists to be the largest source of protein in the world's oceans and is, not surprisingly, an important food source for many organisms.
Although herring are opportunistic feeders, they feed primarily on small holoplankton crustaceans called Copepods. Herring growth rates vary with copepod availably and abundance. In addition to being caught and killed by man in his quest for food, the survival and distribution of herring largely depends on the distribution of their major prey, the copepods. Some of the copepod species make up more than two thirds of the herring's diet in winter. Research has found that herring time their migration patterns around the presence of the copepod, one of which and much favoured, is the *Calanus finmarchicus*.
A pelagic shoaling fish, the herring feeds at night near to the surface of the water, following the migrations of zooplankton that inhabit deeper waters by day and surface waters by night. Herring consume food by using their gill rakers to filter feed. In addition to man and some sea birds, the herring and their eggs have many enemies in the ocean and it could be said that it is eaten by almost everything! These predators include whales, cod, haddock, hake, dolphin, dogfish and other shark species, tuna, pollock, bass and some types of porpoise. On the sea bed, the eggs are very vulnerable to crabs, whelks, starfish and some flat fish. Cod are known to feed not only on the herring eggs but also on larvae, juvenile and adult herring.
Herring are said to be in season for about two months before they spawn when they are both plump and firm. After spawning however, the fish becomes thin, out of condition, and the flesh breaks easily. Such herring are said to be "spent". When a high proportion of spent fish are in the catch of a fishing vessel, the season would be considered to be over at that fishing ground for the time being. Unlike most fish, the herring lays its eggs at the bottom of the sea where they remain until they are hatched.
Mature fish move towards the spawning grounds as their milt and roe begin to develop and gather in large shoals. The female usually lays 20,000 - 50,000 eggs in 30 - 250 ft. of water where they are fertilised by the male fish. In the North Sea, incubation of the eggs takes between 14 and 20 days depending upon the sea temperature. After hatching, the small fry tend to drift with the current and later move to inshore nursery grounds. After 2½ years they move on to other feeding grounds in deeper water and when 3 years old, they can be considered to be mature fish.
Herring are divided into different stocks that are mainly distinguished by the spawning period and location, size and rate of growth, and migration patterns. In the past it was believed that North Atlantic herring were all part of the same stock, and migrated across wide reaches from Iceland in the north to the English Channel and Ireland in the south.

Herring have traditionally been found in vast numbers in the seas around the British Isles and as the stocks of herring on the various fishing grounds spawned at different times, it was in season for most of the year. Much still has to be learnt about the migratory pattern of the herring, which remains an important commercial species for the British fishing industry. It was known to be a predictable fish as it turned up in great quantities at the same time and location each year, however, during any fishery the size of the catch could fluctuate considerably from year to year. On some grounds the fish may spawn in spring, at others they may spawn in the autumn. It is this difference in spawning times which gives rise to the different herring seasons round our coasts. In the past, the major herring drift net fisheries on the east coast of the British

Isles were as shown on the following map:

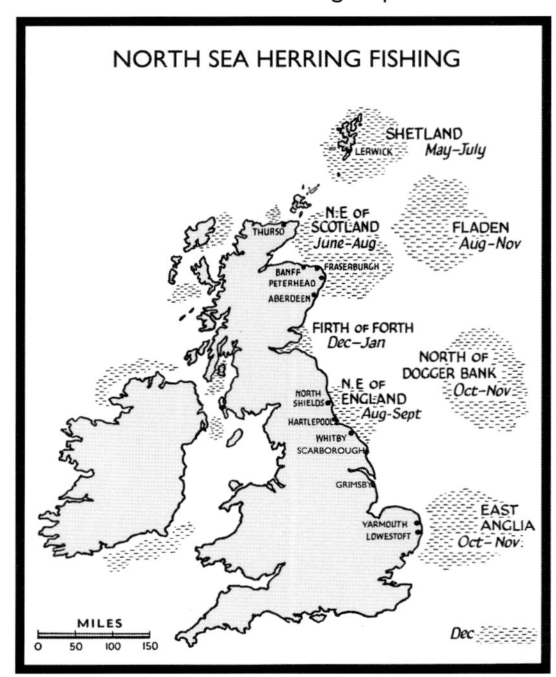

The East Anglian towns of Great Yarmouth, Lowestoft and Southwold can all claim that they were founded upon the harvest of the sea and went on to have harbours that were heavily used in the autumn herring fishery. At one time all three saw large numbers of fishing vessels arrive from Scotland together with a large workforce for this long running annual event. Fishing has been an industry for at least 1000 years in these parts, and continues in the 21st century, but on a greatly reduced scale. Today, longshore and inshore fishing boats working from the ports of Southwold, Lowestoft and Great Yarmouth catch longshore herring when in season. Some small craft still operate from the local beaches and also catch longshore herring, which tend to stay close to the shore.

Vessels used during the East Anglian herring fishery were sail, steam, motor, and in more recent times, diesel powered herring drifters. A typical drifter would have a crew of ten made up of the skipper, mate, hawseman, net stower, whaleman, engineer, stoker, cook and two others. The method of fishing was with nets that drifted with wind and tide, hence the vessels were referred to as "drifters". Starting at the Shetland Islands in the month of May many drifters would fish the different fishing grounds in turn and eventually finish off the year at the East Anglian fishing grounds, in October, November and December. The East Anglian herring fishery produced the very finest quality herrings, full of spawn and of a high nutritional value. Many fish were caught within a relatively short steaming distance on fishing grounds around the Smith's Knoll and from ten to thirty miles abreast of Yarmouth and Lowestoft.

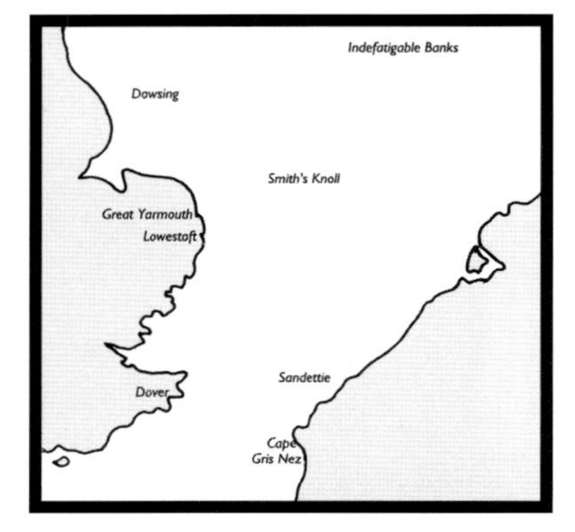

Map showing the Smith's Knoll, Dowsing and Indefatigable, Sandettie and Cape Gris Nez fishing grounds

Traditionally it was thought that the whole species made an annual migratory movement around the British Isles after arriving from a far away place. The reasoning behind this was that herring shoals appeared in northern Scottish waters in early summer and in succession appeared to gradually travel south ending the year in the southern North Sea and English Channel. Many disbelieved the theory of hundreds of fishing vessels following the same fish down the east coast and instead were convinced that different stocks of herring spawned at different locations each year at a different time.

The majority of herring landed in the British Isles are between 8 and 15 inches in length, with the body being deeper than it is thick. The length is around five times the greatest depth of the body. Herring are found on both sides of the north Atlantic with the most important fishing grounds being those off the coast of Canada, Iceland, Norway and Britain. Those caught in the waters off Canada, Iceland and Norway are often larger than the herring caught in the North Sea. In recent years around 90% of the herring landed in the United Kingdom (UK) came from waters around the coasts of Scotland and Northern Ireland.

Only limited fisheries exist in the southern North Sea now, one example being the Thames Blackwater Drift Net fishery, the TAC (total allowable catch limit) being monitored by the Department for the Environment, Food and Rural Affairs. This fishery, for spring spawning herring, is located in the Greater Thames Estuary and is within the UK six-mile limit. It gained much publicity in December 2005 as it became the first fishery that for two years running had been certified as meeting the Marine Stewardship Council's (MSC) environmental standard for sustainable and well-managed fisheries. The Chief Executive of the MSC, Mr. Rupert Howes, stated, "it is very encouraging to see this historic fishery renew its commitment to the MSC process. This is the first fishery to complete the re-assessment process, and we hope that a second five-year period of independent verification of sustainability will be a springboard to future development". The herring, caught in what many consider to be East Anglian waters, have been sold in supermarkets such as Tesco, Sainsbury and Waitrose, in addition to local fishmonger outlets. It is also used in quality fish patés.

The total collapse of the already declining herring stocks in the southern North Sea during the 1960s had a substantial effect on the economies of both Great Yarmouth and Lowestoft. Clear signs of considerable over fishing for many years leading to the virtual destruction of the spawning herring shoals, and possibly some adverse environmental conditions are thought to have been the cause. A most noticeable drop in the quantity of fish being landed occurred between 1954 and 1955 when at Yarmouth alone, the landings fell from 143,622 tons to 63,354 tons. By 1967 the total landings at Yarmouth were only 2,600 tons. During the 1913 season, 824,213 tons of herring had been landed there. Gradual disappearance of the herring shoals and the corresponding lack of opportunities to make good money, lead to fewer drifters participated in the East Anglian autumn herring fishery. Scottish herring drifters had always far out numbered English drifters in the fishery and with disappointing returns returned home early with some trying their luck on the west coast. Others did not bother to make the journey south after hearing of the poor fishing. One aspect of the last few years of the fishery was that due to the greatly reduced number of drifters taking part, the price being paid for the herring that were landed, tended to be very good. Much support was given to the belief that large vessels from other nations using fishing techniques other than drift nets were catching herring at all stages of maturity, often for industrial purposes, leading to wholesale destruction of the stock. Extensive survey work for offshore oil and gas in the southern North Sea started in the early 1960s with some of this work requiring the use of underwater explosive charges. This was considered another factor in the disappearance of the herring shoals from the fishing grounds traditionally worked by drifters based at Great Yarmouth and Lowestoft.

A number of licensing orders, seasonal closures and quota restrictions have been put in place covering the North Sea and other waters in a bid to protect the remaining stock from further over exploitation, but large scale herring fishing from the East Anglian ports is now a distant memory and the herring drifters, those distinct, seaworthy vessels, so much part of the local scene for many years, have now passed into history.

Following a co-ordinated effort, which involved imposing the restrictions already mentioned on herring fishing, the stock has built up again and a good recovery has been seen in some waters. During December 2005, Norway and the European Union (EU) reached agreement on the regulation of the fishery for Norwegian spring-spawning herring in 2006. Norway would fish 564,200 tonnes of herring and the EU only 62,000 tonnes and no EU fishing vessel would be allowed to land herring in Norway. The Norwegians are ensuring that this herring fishery is not over exploited. Unfortunately, unlike Norway, Britain is no longer in a position to control herring fishing since the waters around the country are effectively EU controlled. In addition, the Norwegians have reached an agreement with Russia over the herring fishing. During 2005, the northern North Sea herring fishery was stated as "excellent" with prices for the fish double that in 2004. In August 2005, a representative of the Scottish Pelagic Fisherman's Association was quoted as saying that fishermen from the Scottish ports found no difficulty in filling their allowable herring quota with good sized quality fish. Due to the measures now being taken to protect the herring stocks, it is hoped that the harvest of this much in demand fish can be kept at a sustainable level. Whilst a recovery has taken place in the north, there is apparently no sign of this happened in the southern North Sea. With restrictions on quotas, and the building of new fishing vessels, together with high running costs, there seems very little prospect that Yarmouth and Lowestoft can ever be important fishing centres again.

Drift Net Fishing

During the East Anglian autumn fishery, the Scottish and English drifters caught the herring by using drift nets. In addition to herring, other pelagic species as sprats, pilchards, and mackerel could also be caught by this method. Drift nets hung at or just below the surface in a vertical wall of netting rather like an extensive curtain at a location where the fish were likely to be. Depending upon which species are being fished, will determine whether the nets are at or beneath the surface.

When herring fishing, each drifter could carry between 70-120 nets, depending on the size of the vessel. Made of cotton, each net was 40-60 yards long and approximately 10 yards deep, thus making the wall of netting at least 2 miles long for a fleet of nets. The drifters would leave the harbour so as to be on the fishing grounds before sunset. Once there, the use of an echo sounder would help the skipper of the drifter determine where the herring shoals were. Before the days of the echo sounder a skipper needed great skill and experience in successfully deciding were to cast his nets. Indications of the presence of herring shoals included the colour of the water, swooping gulls, diving gannets and spouting whales.

If the echo sounder indicated good prospects for a profitable catch, the crew would pay out the fleet of nets over the side of the drifter after the vessel had been turned so that she was sailing with the wind. The echo sounder determined the distance between the keel of the drifter and the seabed and detected shoals of herring. On early echo sounders, the output of this electronic instrument was recorded continuously by means of a swinging needle on a strip of paper. With all the nets in the water, the drifter's mizzen sail would be set taut to keep her head into the wind.

The drift nets would be suspended in the water at one or two fathoms (6-12 feet) below the surface. To maintain the nets in a vertical position each net had a large number of corks along the headline at the top. To the headline were attached buffs (large hide, canvas or plastic buoys). The bottom of the nets was kept down by attaching them to a heavy rope, known as a warp, messenger, leader or buss rope. This warp pulled the nets down to their full width, acted as a strengthening rope and was the main means of attachment to the drifter. To help preserve the nets they were periodically boiled in Acacia Catechu (an extract from an East Indian tree) whilst at the net store and then allowed to dry on drying rails or spread out on the ground. The nets were continuously checked for tears and other damage to see if they needed replacing or required the attention of beatsters either at the net store or in the home of one these ladies. The work of the beatster involved spending many hours standing with long spells of continuous alertness and concentration.

Herring shoals rise during the hours of darkness and if the nets were set in the right area the fish would swim into them with the result that the mature fish would be trapped and prevented from escaping by their gill covers. The size of the net mesh played an important part in the survival of the herring stocks. If it was too small the younger fish would be unable to escape through the net to achieve maturity. On some grounds and at certain times, herring have been caught by the trawl. This method involves hunting and capturing fish by dragging a large net behind a trawler or trawlers. With very few exceptions, it was not a method of fishing traditionally used by vessels engaged in the East Anglian herring fishery and is not considered appropriate for this book.

A steam drifter "hanging on to her nets" on the fishing grounds

The drifter would "hang on to the nets" as she and the nets drifted with the wind and tide in the darkness for a period of between four and six hours or perhaps longer.
On a moonlit night the view from a drifter's wheelhouse was of a line of buoys (buffs) bobbing about and disappearing into the distance. When hauling the nets in, an indication of the size of catch was sometimes given by the amount of fish in the first two or three nets. Using the drifter's steam or electric capstan, hauling would commence if the skipper was satisfied that the "show" of herring in the nets was good. The nets were manhandled inboard, the herring shaken out on deck and then passed down through the fish scuttles into the fish room and the lockers for storage. The drifter would then return to port if the skipper considered the catch sufficient; but landing the fish the next day would probably mean lower prices. Upon reaching port, the drifter's catch would be transferred to the shore using a quarter cran basket. This basket held at least 250 fish and was swung between the drifter and the shore by means of the drifter's derrick, or cran pole.

The time taken in hauling the nets on board a drifter varied with the amount of fish in the nets and the weather at the time. A catch of 50 crans could take around four hours for the crew to haul in the whole fleet of nets. A catch of over 200 crans could take as long as 18 hours of non-stop hard work for the crew hauling the nets inboard.

The official cran measure, introduced in 1908, is now to be found in the Lowestoft Maritime Museum and is stated in British Imperial measures and given as 37½ gallons, 28 stones by weight or approximately 1320 herring, depending on fish size. Before the introduction of the cran measure, herring were counted out by hand on the drifter or market as follows:

Four herrings = Warp
132 herrings = Long hundred of herring
1320 herrings = Ten hundred herring

With all the nets, buffs and gear safely recovered from the sea, the drifter would head for Great Yarmouth, Lowestoft, and, prior to the First World War, Southwold as quickly as possible to discharge the catch, and then probably return immediately to the fishing grounds after taking on board stores.

Selling and Fish Processing

As herring do not keep well, it was important to get them to market as quickly as possible and sold in a herring auction in the saleroom. Firms that processed herrings for the different markets tried if possible to have the fish processed, or to start processing before they had been out of the water for 24 hours.
Immediately a drifter arrives in port, a sample of the catch of around 20-30 fish would be taken to the sale room where the auctioneer shows the sample, and tells the buyers the estimated size of the catch. The fish is then sold with the various buyers bidding against each other to buy the herring. During some herring seasons, the price paid by the trade was regulated with a minimum and maximum allowable value put on the fish in order to satisfy supply and demand conditions. Fish that a buyer had bid for and won, would be collected from the quayside after being off loaded from the drifter and put into boxes or containers for transport to the buyers yard, pickling plot, herring station or other premises. At this point, buyers have been known to dispute the quality of the fish purchased when compared against the quality of the sample seen at auction. The best of the fish would go for freshing, smoking, salting, marinating or canning, and the poorer quality would go for pet food, fertiliser, fish meal, or used as a source of oil.
For many years it was normal for tens of millions of herring to be caught each season and a vast industry with a major Scottish input was engaged in preserving the fish so that they could be eaten long after being caught. Some local elements of this extensive industry still exist and are in daily use as they carry out the same functions as they have done for generations in preserving herring the traditional way. The great majority of herring processed locally in the 21st century are transported hundreds of miles to East Anglia, the only herring landed locally being small quantities of longshore fish caught by the inshore and longshore boats.
Many different names have been applied to the herring after being preserved by processes that involve smoking, salting or by a combination of both. These include bloaters, buckling, cured herring, kippers, and red herring. Another form of preserving the fish for future consumption was by canning, where the herring was packed in cans which were usually filled with tomato sauce. The can was then closed and heat processed. Vast numbers of herring

passed through the now closed local canneries with annual quantities of 12 million being typically processed, packed and dispatched to markets around the world. Fresh unprocessed herring has been, and continues to be available in fishmongers, supermarkets and other outlets, but traditionally the main use of the fish has been in smoked, cured, marinated and canned products. The kipper is by far the most important and well known smoked herring product and is widely available to the consumer in both pre-packed, and basic forms through supermarkets and fishmongers. It is produced by cold smoking herring that have been split down the back, gutted and had the roe removed, cleaned, steeped in brine, and for some markets treated with a vegetable dye. The herring are then smoked for periods varying from 8-16 hours over fires of oak shavings and damp sawdust in a traditional smokehouse. Within the smokehouse the herring, are hung on tenterhooks attached to horizontal beams. The roof has louvres or roof openings allowing the smoke to escape and the free circulation of air. Air circulation is important since without it the kipper could became dry and unpalatable. By using a mechanical kiln, the smoking period can be reduced considerably although many say the flavour is impaired by this method. Bloaters are whole herring, dry salted or immersed in brine, dried overnight in a smoke house, and slightly cold smoked. Buckling is herring with the head and gut removed, brined and then hot smoked. Red herring or High Dries are whole ungutted herring, heavily salted and cold smoked for 2-3 weeks or longer. This hard cured fish is exported to Mediterranean countries. Cold smoking usually means a temperature of 26°- 32°C and hot smoking, a temperature of 76°-82°C. Some herring were, and still are, marinated, this is a process of preserving the fish in a mixture of acetic acid and salt. Products such as rollmops are fillets of herring treated in this way, they have a limited shelf life and are known in the trade as semipreserves.

Other East Anglian produced herring products much in demand include Buckling Pate, Kipper Pate, Bloater Pate and Herring Roe Pate. At the time of writing (2006), at least six traditional smokehouses are in daily use in East Anglian coastal towns using the time honoured method of processing, and one non functioning herring curing works now forms part of a museum at Great Yarmouth where visitors are shown dummy herring hung up, and waiting to be smoked.

Perhaps the most memorable scenes of the autumn herring season at Yarmouth, Gorleston, Lowestoft and Southwold were quaysides crowded with herring drifters and large areas of land in each town taken over for pickling plots where Scottish lasses would gut and pack herring in barrels to produce pickle cured herring. This was an immense operation in the days of the fishery, with thousands of Scottish folk making the annual journey to the ports to process the herring landed there. When the herring arrived at the pickling plot or curers yard from the quayside they were emptied into troughs or "farlanes" and sprinkled with salt. A farlane was about 4 feet wide and usually ran the length of the plot or curing yard. A team of three, usually ladies, formed of two gutters and one packer would set about gutting the fish and placing them into a rousing tub or trough where each fish is coated in salt. The packer would put the herring in layers in barrels, separating each layer with a quantity of salt. The salt extracted moisture from the fish and brine was formed: this penetrated all the tissues of the fish and acted as a preservative, the amount of salt used depended on the type of "cure" required. A cooper then put the lid on the barrel and it was left for a while to settle. The lid was then removed by the cooper and a hole drilled near to the bottom of the barrel which allowed the blood pickle to run into a container. The barrel was then top tiered with more herring and closed, tilted on its side and refilled with some of the pickle drawn off earlier. The hole was plugged and the barrel of pickled cured herring was then ready for final inspection and dispatch to continental markets by cargo steamer.

The autumn herring fishery, the annual visit to East Anglia by hundreds of Scottish drifters and thousands of Scottish workers is no more, but some of the interesting infrastructure and buildings relating to this great bygone event can still be found at Caister, Yarmouth, Gorleston, Lowestoft, Kessingland, Southwold and other coastal towns and villages. Buildings used for smokehouses, fishing gear storage, curing establishments and maintaining drift nets all had a unique character, and today these are easy to identify although now in use for different purposes. On the North Denes at Lowestoft, a large area has net drying rails and posts in position and on the adjacent Whapload Road many buildings associated with the herring fishing exist together with one of the finest fishing museums in the UK.

YEAR	HERRINGS LANDED	YEAR	HERRINGS LANDED
1893	16,184 Lasts	1932	279,230 Crans
1894	24,441 "	1933	294,575 "
1895	17,588 "	1934	274,052 "
1896	19,250 "	1935	335,899 "
1897	23,013 "	1936	324,747 "
1898	19,056 "	1937	372,604 "
1899	26,960 "	1938	303,083 "
1900	29,000 "	1939	107,560 "
1901	29,646 "	1940	No Fishing
1902	45,323 "	1941	" "
1903	39,798 "	1942	" "
1904	40,943 "	1943	" "
1905	38,505 "	1944	" "
1906	35,050 "	1945	92,875 Crans
1907	52,120 "	1946	220,716 "
1908	44,546 "	1947	239,708 "
1909	44,267 "	1948	294,413 "
1910	34,872 "	1949	178,154 "
1911	523,335 Crans	1950	191,652 "
1912	683,574 "	1951	188,753 "
1913	824,213 "	1952	136,073 "
1914	177,459 "	1953	149,704 "
1915	120,122 "	1954	143,622 "
1916	12,289 "	1955	63,354 "
1917	77,782 "	1956	61,114 "
1918	202,485 "	1957	73,455 "
1919	453,571 "	1958	35,098 "
1920	616,806 "	1959	28,120 "
1921	358,573 "	1960	19,781 "
1922	342,237 "	1961	33,873 "
1923	389,164 "	1962	21,172 "
1924	654,982 "	1963	19,391 "
1925	479,293 "	1964	19,203 "
1926	393,380 "	1965	12,657 "
1927	406,366 "	1966	9,657 "
1928	522,419 "	1967	2,600 "
1929	528,513 "	1968	810 "
1930	540,665 "	1969	NIL
1931	390,352 "	1970	71 Crans

SUMMARY OF HERRINGS LANDED
AT
YARMOUTH
1893-1970

Herring counted by hand
(prior to 1910)

One last = 100 long hundreds
Long Hundred =132 herrings

Herring measured in crans

The official cran measure is approximately 1,320 herrings, 28 Imperial stones of fish or 37½ Imperial gallons of fish

The official cran measure can be seen in the Lowestoft Maritime Museum where a great many other artefacts relating to the herring fishery can be seen including the celebrated Prunier Herring Trophy.

This scene at Gorleston demonstrates how heavily involved it was during the herring fishing, with drifters landing their catches there and the area having curing yards and pickling plots. Many owners had net stores and other buildings used for the storage and maintenance of fishing gear in Gorleston and a number of fish and smoke houses were also to be found there. With Peterhead drifters landing their catches on the Gorleston side of the river, two steamers can be seen on the Yarmouth side, possibly taking barrels of cured herring away or bringing empty barrels to Yarmouth from Scotland. Scottish fisher girls can be seen gutting and packing herring in barrels on the centre right of the photograph in the curing yard. *(MWC)*

Another Gorleston scene showing drifters landing their catches and piles of swills on the quay. The nearest of the two drifters is YH997 *Girl Winifred*, with YH172 *Ocean Emperor* partly obscured by the swills. The swill, which held 500-600 herrings, was only used at Yarmouth and Gorleston. The fishing registry for the *Girl Winifred* closed on 3rd September 1951 and she was broken up. The registry for *Ocean Emperor* was closed in May 1948 and she then passed to the Sea Cadets for used as a headquarters ship. *Ocean Emperor* was eventually dumped on the south side of Breydon Water. *(MWC)*

A view from 1905 at Gorleston as the steam drifter YH828 *Blackthorn*, built in 1904 at Smith's Dock , North Shields and owned by Westmacott Ltd., heads for sea. Sold in 1932 to Banff, she was scrapped in 1936.(*MWC*)

Southwold has been involved with the herring industry for around 1000 years and during the 18th century was a base for the Dutch in their robust and sea worthy fishing vessels, the "buss".
The 1890s saw plans made for rebuilding the harbour into a modern fishing port with all necessary facilities.
This scene at Southwold shows many of the town's fishing boats drawn up on the beach in front of the town during the 1890s.
Southwold still has many inshore fishing boats operating from the harbour. (*MWC*)

Construction of the new road and the large herring sale ring, similar to those at Lowestoft and Yarmouth, was well advanced at Southwold when this view was recorded in 1906. (*DMC*)

In 1907, the rebuilt harbour at Southwold opened and before long it became a busy herring port with two types of Scottish sailing drifters, the "Fifies" and "Zulus", being based there for the season together with steam drifters. This scene, recorded during the autumn herring season of 1908, shows Scottish fisher girls gutting herring down by the harbour, with the newly completed market and saleroom in the background. There are plenty of herring in the "Farlane", indicating that the Southwold based Scottish drifters are finding good shoals out in the North Sea. (*DMC*)

Recorded in the early 1900s, the crew of a Scottish sailing drifter are seen landing their catch with the aid of the steam capstan. Although not powered by steam, many sailing drifters, both Scottish and English, had steam capstans that could be used for a variety of purpose, but mainly for hauling in the drift net warp. (*PKC*)

A 1905 view of the fish wharf at Yarmouth with swills being filled with herring, and sailing drifters at the quay. (*MWC*)

A pile of fish such as this was a common sight around the time of the First World War when the herring fishing was at its height. Often large amounts of herring were left unsold when the supply exceeded the demand and were dumped on nearby fields. This scene was recorded in 1912 at the Waveney Dock in Lowestoft. *(MWC)*

An example of conditions on a typical pickling plot in the early 1920s with the ground a mass of mud created by rain, fish juices, blood and horse droppings all churned up by numerous horses and carts, and people walking about. The area seen here is close to what was know locally as the "beach village", a self contained community of fishing folk that had shops, a post office, public houses, a bakery and other facilities. The complete village, so much part of the local fishing heritage, was demolished in the 1960s. *(PKC)*

A large number of steam drifters, all of which appear to be Scottish, entering the harbour at Yarmouth in the 1930s, with PD604 *Nellie McGee*, built at Govan in 1908, in the prominent position in the photograph. (*PKC*)

With fish scales seemingly everywhere, six members of the crew of a Scottish steam drifter stop cleaning their nets for a moment for the photographer at Yarmouth in 1913. The steam drifter laying alongside is BCK98 *Campania*, built in 1907 at Sandhaven and owned by P. Cormack and associates, of Portgordon. (*MWC*)

The barrel was one of the important items in the herring processing industry and many coopers were employed at all three ports making them, in addition to hundreds of barrels shipped down from Scotland. Coopers are seen here making barrels at Lowestoft that have the top and bottom hoops made of medal and the others made of wood, mainly ash. *(PKC)*

Cork cutting was one of the many skilled and vital jobs associated with the herring fishing industry that have disappeared. Three chaps are seen here in 1913 making and shaping various types of corks out of blocks for use with drift nets. *(MWC)*

Crowds of people are watching the activities aboard the mainly Scottish drifters in this attractive scene at Southwold where both sailing and steam vessels are at the quay. In the distance can be seen the funnel of the port tug. The barrels on the right appear to be empty and are waiting to be filled with herring by the Scotch fisher girls, many of whom stayed in lodgings across the river at Walberswick in addition to those staying in Southwold. (*DMC*)

Large areas of land at all three ports were set aside for use in the autumn and winter for pickling plots. Scotch fisher girls are seen here at Yarmouth sorting into different sizes, and gutting herring at the farlanes. In the background, hundreds of barrels are stored prior to being filled with herring, usually for markets abroad. (*MWC*)

Before the introduction of the aluminium trunk in the 1950s, various types of baskets and wooden boxes were used throughout the herring industry and both box makers and basket makers were in great demand. These chaps at work in a store in Lowestoft are making baskets using locally grown osier, which is any type of willow tree or shrub cultivated for the supple and pliable twigs and branches it has. *(MWC)*

The repair and maintenance of drifter's nets was a time consuming but vital task. "Ransackers" and "beatsters" were responsible for the inspection and repair of any damage the nets sustained during fishing. Ransackers were tasked with the inspection of the drift nets, and the beatsters repaired any damage found. Beatsters are seen here at work in a Lowestoft net store repairing nets in the late 1940s. Many beatsters, including the author's mother, repaired nets at home. *(MWC)*

The North Denes and Whapload Road at Lowestoft were traditionally associated with the fishing industry and today many buildings associated with that trade remain, although used for other purposes. The Denes were used for drying drift nets and the net stores and beating chambers such as those in the background, are where the nets and fishing gear would have been maintained. The smoke from the chimney indicates that the copper is alight, ready for nets to be dipped in hot cutch which would help to preserve them. (*MWC*)

Often forgotten are the living conditions at sea for the people who made the herring industry possible. Before the days of electric light, this crew of a steam drifter appear to be enjoying their somewhat basic meal. (*MWC*)

Mr. John Woodger, a Newcastle man, apparently discovered by accident the process of making kippers in 1843 at Seahouses. This scene in a local smokehouse shows herring, after being split, gutted and lightly salted, being placed ready for smoking above burning heaps of oak shavings and sawdust. For some markets, the fish can stay in the smoke for periods of up to 16 hours. The herring are hanging on tenterhooks that are fastened to battens. These battens are hung in tiers on racks inside the smokehouse over the burning shavings and sawdust. With many traditional smoke houses remaining in daily use in 2006, the work of the smoker is very much a current occupation. *(PTP)*

Following a technique mastered by the Dutch in the 16th century, herring are packed in a barrel by a Scots fisher girl after being gutted and salted. Each layer of herrings was separated by a layer of salt. As part of this process of curing, the salt and the fish liquids produce a blood pickle that preserves the herring. Scottish lasses did the gutting and packing, and men worked as coopers and carters. *(PKC)*

A view inside the herring sale ring at the Waveney Dock in Lowestoft during the 1930s, with buyers examining a sample of herring from a drifter's catch prior to the auction. The box of herring can be seen in the lower centre of the photograph. (*MWC*)

In later years, auctions were often held on the quayside and on 13th October 1969, George Thom, in the centre of the photograph, is selling herring landed at Lowestoft by one of the few Scottish drifters still visiting East Anglia at that time. (*PTP*)

A fine study of Scottish steam and motor powered drifters at Yarmouth in the 1930s. The Yarmouth longshore boat in the foreground is YH436 *Ellen*. The round building on the right in front of the drifters is the fish sale ring. (*PKC*)

Another comprehensive and unusual view of drifters at Yarmouth. As in the above scene, all the drifters that can be identified are Scottish. The vital railway tramway that connected the port area to the national rail network via Yarmouth Vauxhall and Beach stations is seen. This allowed vast tonnages of coal and salt to be delivered to the drifters, the port area and other vessels direct from the mines, and also carried immense quantities of fish and other products direct to inland markets from Yarmouth. In recent times, with no foreseeable use for the rail link it was taken up, and all goods and freight to the port area are carried by road through Great Yarmouth. The herring industry at Lowestoft and Southwold, also dispatched fish and received coal and salt by the railway. (*PKC*)

With the warp coming on board through the molgogger at the bow of YH296 *Ocean Hunter*, the crew haul the nets on board the drifter. The molgogger or mole-jenny was a portable device consisting of vertical and horizontal rollers that could be moved to various positions on a drifter. However, it was usually placed near the bows of the vessel as seen here. One of the many buffs is floating in the sea by the side of *Ocean Hunter* waiting to be recovered from the water. Built as the Admiralty steam drifter HMD *Current* in 1919, *Ocean Hunter* joined the Yarmouth fleet in 1948 after purchase by Bloomfields as the *Copious*. She was renamed *Ocean Hunter* on 25th March 1948. In 1952, *Ocean Hunter* was sold to well known Lowestoft owner Edward Beamish and given the new port letters and fishing number of LT322. She was sold for scrapping in 1955. (*LESMS*).

A good illustration of the weight of fish the nets used by drifters had to bear when the nets are out of the water and well filled with herring. The crew of a wooden steam drifter built by John Chambers Ltd. are seen here hauling the nets on board. (*PKC*)

The view from a drifter of the buffs and corks supporting the nets as they are hauled in. On the left of the photograph, another drifter can be seen on the fishing grounds some miles away. (*LESMS*)

To help with the manhandling of the nets as they came on board, they passed over a portable roller fixed on the sides of the drifter. This view shows the roller in use when the nets were hauled in by hand. (*LESMS*)

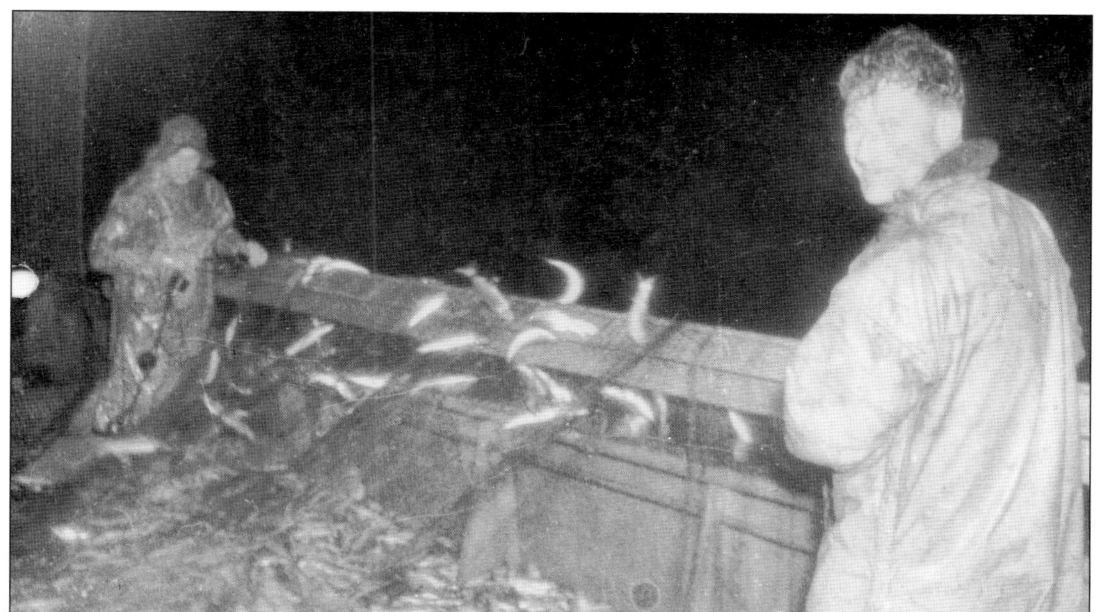

In 1948, powered rollers were installed on the drifter LT371 *Dauntless Star.* When this scene was recorded over 18 tons of herrings had been brought on board in just over 3 hours with the powered roller. The rollers made a tremendous difference to the crew by reducing the hours of toil usually associated with hauling in the nets, but were not suitable for many drifters and the use of the powered rollers was limited. (*LESMS*)

Maintenance of fishing gear is ongoing as this unusual view of the drifter FR178 *Silver Harvest* at Yarmouth demonstrates, with buffs hung up for checking and some having been freshly painted. (*MWC*)

Everyday sights associated with the herring industry were taken for granted for so long in East Anglia but are now no more. Sundays excepted, this once daily routine of the crew of a Scottish motor drifter bringing ashore the drifter's catch at Yarmouth or Lowestoft was so common in the herring season few people took note of what was happening.
These gentlemen were recorded at Lowestoft in Hamilton Dock in the 1950s. Numerous plans have been put forward for the future use of this and the other docks with yacht marinas being the favourite. Hamilton Dock is nowadays used by the remaining inshore fishing boats. *(PTP)*

Wooden steam drifters have long passed into history. Of the hundreds built, not one has been preserved although the remains of a number still exist, examples being at Lowestoft and in the Falkland Islands.
With smoke from her funnel drifting across the camera lens, YH927 *Ma Freen* leaves Yarmouth for the fishing grounds. This fine example was built at the John Chambers shipyard at Lowestoft in 1913 and was fitted with a 25nhp triple expansion engine made by Elliott and Garrood of Beccles, who also made her boiler. After being hit by another drifter whilst moored at Yarmouth on 25th October 1938, *Ma Freen* sank but was raised and put on the Spending Beach. She was later broken up and her registry closed in May 1939. *(MWC)*

Drifters

Before the introduction of steam, motor and diesel powered craft, the sailing vessels used during the autumn East Anglian herring fishery by the English included dandies, luggers, drifters or converter smacks (able to drift net fish for herring, and to trawl for white fish). The vast visiting Scottish sailing fleets consisted of "fifies", which had a straight stem and stern, or "zulus" which had a straight stem and a raked stern.

LT247 *Contest*-an English sailing drifter
(*MWC*)

The decline in the large number of sail powered herring catching craft started in the 1890s and early 1900s after the first steam engine had been tried successfully in a herring fishing vessel in the late 1870s. This new power source gave the vessel greater independence of the elements and generally enabled it to achieve a higher speed in travelling to and from the fishing grounds. Steam power had been used for some years in sailing vessels to drive capstans and auxiliaries.

No successful commercial steam fishing vessels were in operation in 1875, but over the next seven years a number of steam paddle tugs were converted to enable them to tow a trawl net along the seabed and the first steam powered purpose built fishing vessels appeared. The paddle tugs were used extensively at various ports to tow sailing vessels of all types in and out of harbour, and it became obvious to some skippers that if the tug was towing a sailing drifter or trawler to sea to go fishing, then why not do the fishing with the tug thereby giving greater independence, power and flexibility. One disadvantage was the cost of the coal they burnt, the sailing vessels being powered by free wind! Another was that the paddle tugs were intended to work in and around harbours and were not suited to working on the fishing grounds in rough weather many miles offshore. By the late 1880s, some fishing ports had embarked upon the replacement of sailing trawlers by purpose built propeller driven steam trawlers and Hull, with access nearby to relatively cheap coal, became the first English port by the early 1900s to completely dispense with sailing trawlers. At some ports with the coalfields many miles away, thus necessitating expensive coal haulage costs, the sailing trawlers were still in use well into the 1930s.

The herring fishing industry was somewhat slower in switching over to steam power, but once the general trend started in the late 1890s it accelerated and hundreds of propeller driven steam herring drifters appeared with builders constructing them as fast as possible. Many consider that the first purpose built steam drifter was the LH880 *Onward,* designed by Mr. David Allan and constructed in 1877 at Leith, and registered there in 1878. The *Onward* was built of wood, just over 56 feet long and powered by a 16hp engine. She had a crew of seven men and a boy, and was initially owned by the Forth Steam Fishing Co. Ltd. Mr. Allan died at South Shields in 1925 at the age of 72, and was considered by many to be the founder of the steam fishing industry. Another early steam fishing vessel was the *Rob Roy*, which was launched in 1882 and also registered at Leith. She looked very similar to the *Onward,* but had a different stern assembly.

The very first steam powered drifter built at Lowestoft was the *Consolation*, built by Chambers and Colby in 1897 for Mr. G. Catchpole of Kessingland. The Catchpole family have a long and much respected association with the East Anglian fishing industry and over the years owned many steam and diesel powered drift-ers and trawlers. *Consolation* was fitted with a 15hp two cylinder compound condensing engine manufactured by Elliott and Garrood at Beccles, a firm that went on to become well known as leading manufacturers of a wide range of steam plant and machin-ery for marine use including capstans, winches, pumps and boilers as well as engines. The development of the steam drifter was rapid, and only two years after the launch of the wooden hulled *Consolation,* the first steel hulled drifter, the *Claudian* was launched at the Yarmouth shipyard of Fellows and Co. at Southtown.

LT396 *United*-a typical early steam drifter
(*MWC*)

Many steam driven iron hulled vessels had been constructed at various yards during this period but the *Claudian* was destined to be the forerunner of hundreds of steel hulled steam drifters.
The wholesale demise of the sailing drifter was set in motion only after the suspicions of the sailing drifter owners about the new power source had been overcome, and also after they saw how efficient the first steamers were that had been built for the pioneering owners. The high cost of building and running a new steam drifter when the owner already successfully operated a sailing drifter left many wondering if the change was worth the financial outlay. In the early 1900s, at a time when the last of the sailing drifters were being built, the cost of a new vessel was between £500 and £700, whereas a new steam drifter would cost around £2000. However, the steam drifter at approximately 80ft. long, was 20 ft. longer than the sailing counterpart and able to carry more nets. Unlike a trawler, which needs substantial power to carry out the function of dragging a net along the seabed, the drifter only needed power to travel to and from the fishing grounds. However this factor became very important after the first few steam drifters joined the vast number of sailing drifters in the fishing fleets at the many English and Scottish ports. It was usual to return to port from the herring fishing grounds as quickly as possible to land the herring in a fresh condition and get the best price, and for this the steam drifters easily beat the sailing drifters with their consistent higher speed and independence of the wind and tide. An owner operating a number of sailing drifters at a time when other owners were operating the new steam drifters, found himself in a difficult financial position. The steamers generally got to market first and thus achieved a better return on their catch.
Around the same time as the widespread introduction of the steam drifter, internal combustion engines were being installed in a number of sailing fishing vessels, especially in Scotland. Many craft were converted to accommodate the new power source, and before long vessels were being built specifically as motor driven fishing craft. In the years leading up to the First World War these motorised vessels became increasingly common in east coast ports. As with the early steam drifters, many owners retained sails on their vessels for a number of years as a standby against failure of the engine and possibly to use when conditions were favourable in order to reduce fuel consumption.
By 1908, Great Yarmouth, Lowestoft and Southwold were seeing hundreds of steam drifters, a few motor driven craft and a diminishing number of sailing drifters filling the harbours during the herring season. Interestingly, Southwold had a new harbour constructed for the fishing trade which was planned to open in 1907 and in 1908, the first year of operation, 296 Scottish drifters landed over 6,000 tons of fish there. On 3rd November 1908, over twenty drifters entered Southwold harbour from the fishing grounds with large catches but the market was already saturated. The Scottish fisher girls at Southwold were fully committed and some of the drifters left hoping for better prospects of landing and selling their catches at Lowestoft and Great Yarmouth.
During the 1909 fishery, 761 steam and sail powered drifters visited the port but the season was poor with bad weather and dismal catches. The following season saw a dramatic fall in the number of Scottish drifters visiting Southwold and in 1911 the decline continued. By 1913, only a few Scottish drifters ventured to Southwold, leaving the newly built harbour with the locally owned herring drifters still landing their catches there. As at Lowestoft and Great Yarmouth, the town had seen large numbers of Scottish fisher girls working on the pickling plots with a fair number of buyers and curers visiting the town, but the future for the East Anglian autumn herring fishing season was mainly at Great Yarmouth and Lowestoft. Poor marketing opportunities, not enough curers, inadequate infrastructure and the restricted capabilities of the narrow gauge Southwold Railway to carry thousands of tons of fish away from the town to inland markets, together with a new major facility at Lowestoft, the Hamilton Dock, were some of the reasons given for the failure of Southwold to develop as a major

fishing port. Despite these problems, many considered that Southwold was better placed than Great Yarmouth and Lowestoft for herring fishing when the shoals were in the far south of the North Sea.

In 1903, the sailing drifter *Our Boys* was completed for her Yarmouth owner Mr. J. T. Moore and became one of the last of the type built for English owners. By 1912, most Scottish owners had decided that steam propulsion was the way forward and had invested heavily in steam drifters. The years leading up to the First World War saw the herring industry reach its peak with drifters during the 1913 season landing quite remarkable quantities of fish. That season 1,163 steam drifters landed around 835 million herrings, with Monday 12th October being a notable day when at Lowestoft 35 steam drifters each landed over 200 crans (about 264,000 herrings). The 1903 built Lowestoft drifter *Hyacinth*, owned by the Herring Fishing Co. Ltd, was top boat with 310 crans.

Whilst that particular season may have seemed financially rewarding for the owners, they faced enormous expense when having a steam drifter built and heavy landings often meant poor prices for the fish. For the vessel to be cost-effective it was vital to keep it working throughout the year. Herring fishing is seasonal but trawling is not, and in the years immediately prior to the First World War, many drifters were built such that they could easily be converted to trawlers. This new class of fishing vessel, initially 80- 85 feet in length became known as the drifter/trawler and could be considered as the equivalent to the converter smacks in the days of sail. An example of this type of vessel was the *Norfolk County* built in 1908 by Cochrane at Selby for the County Fishing Co. Ltd. In the 1920s, many larger drifter/trawlers were built with the last steam-powered vessels entering service in the early 1930s. The great majority of these were of steel construction, although a few, such as the 1926 Yarmouth built *Renascent* were of wood. As an alternative to converting to trawling when the East Anglian herring fishing season had ended, many drifters would travel to ports such as Newlyn, Milford Haven and Dunmore East (Ireland) early in the year to take part in the local fishery there. During the summer months, some Lowestoft and Yarmouth drifters could often be found working off the west coast of Scotland. During the spring, East Anglian drifters were to be found at North Shields and Hartlepool followed by others making for Lerwick in the Shetlands. Later ports such as Wick, Peterhead, Fraserburgh and Aberdeen played host to the English vessels as they joined the local drifters in the herring fishing. From mid summer until the autumn months, Yarmouth and Lowestoft drifters landed fish at such ports as North Shields, Hartlepool, Scarborough and Grimsby whilst participating in the local herring fishing. This period was followed by the vessels working from approximately October until the end of the year from their home ports of Yarmouth and Lowestoft, after which the cycle would be repeated.

The First World War saw hundreds of drifters and trawlers called upon to undertake naval duties and, after conversion work had been completed, being assigned such work as minesweeping, stores and water carrying, examination work, "net" drifters (to lay a steel indicator net barrage against submarines and other submerged objects), chaplain tenders, mail tenders, cable repair vessels, auxiliary patrol duties, fleet tenders and boom defence vessels. Many requisitioned drifters were lost, together with crew members, during the First World War.

BF74 *Nellie Gardner*-a standard steam drifter in commercial service (*MWC*)

Later during the war, it was planned that the requisitioned drifters were to be supplemented by the building of over 300 Admiralty "standard" drifters. The building programme began in May 1917 when 115 contracts were placed with different shipbuilding yards for the construction of vessels built to a standard wooden design based on the 420 class built by John Chambers Ltd. at Lowestoft. A further batch of 165 steel vessels were ordered from a number of yards, the design being based on the steam drifter *Ocean Reward*, a product of Alexander Hall of Aberdeen. As part of the war effort a further 100 wooden drifters, built to the "standard" design, were constructed in Canada having been ordered in January 1917. These were all launched during 1917. Due to their late inception and production difficulties, the war service given by both British and Canadian built "standard" drifters was limited, but some did enter the auxiliary patrol service whilst others became minesweepers and fleet tenders.

After the war, a great many of the newly built standard drifters, some without ever entering naval service, were sold by Admiralty agents to fishing vessel owners. Several spent periods laid up and for sale at Lowestoft. The *Groundswell* (Admiralty No. 4137) was an example of a "standard" drifter sold by the Admiralty to a fishing company, subsequently becoming the Lowestoft drifter *Elie Ness*.

With the war over, many expected the East Anglian autumn herring fishery to be as productive as the record breaking 1913 season had been, and as a result of this, during the 1920 season, over 1100 drifters participated in the fishery. Unfortunately this optimism was ill founded, the amount of fish being caught was not as great as expected and the market was suffering badly from post war depression together with the near collapse of the valuable herring export market to Russia, Germany and countries in Eastern Europe. This made it very difficult for the drifter owners, skippers and the crew to make much money.

Despite the vast numbers of steam drifters involved in the British herring industry, the development of the more efficient, cleaner and easier to work motor powered drifters continued, especially in Scotland. At the commencement of the Second World War demands were again made upon the fishing industry to provide drifters and trawlers to cover naval duties. As in the First World War, fishing vessels were requisitioned, and again these were to be supplemented by a large number of vessels built to an Admiralty specification by many different yards in the UK. These vessels, known as Motor Fishing Vessels (MFVs), were designed such that once the war was over; they could be sold by the Admiralty and easily converted to fishing vessels by their new owners, a similar scenario to that of the standard steam drifters of the First World War.

Between 1939 and 1945, 109 steam drifters in Admiralty service were lost through mines, collisions, groundings, working in wild seas, attacks by enemy aircraft, enemy gunfire and at Dunkirk,

Steam drifters at Lowestoft after being returned by the Admiralty following the end of the war. (*PKC*)

MFV *1219*-An Admiralty MFV
(*MWC*)

where wrecks near the beaches proved a severe hazard and German aircraft and coastal gun batteries did all they could to destroy any allied ship. English and Scottish drifters and their crews paid a heavy price before peace finally came to these shores in 1945.

Once peace had returned to the North Sea, the herring industry started to get back to normal, but with many drifters lost and others in a run down and badly neglected state, much work was needed to regain the position that existed before the war. A great many Scottish owners purchased surplus MFVs from the Admiralty to replace worn out and increasingly expensive to run steam drifters. In the early 1950s, the estimated running costs per week for a Scottish motor drifter was calculated at £60-£70, and for a steam drifter it was £120. With such a substantial difference, the advantages of finishing with steam were obvious and with many reasonably priced surplus Admiralty MFVs available, the choice was quite clear. New diesel powered drifters were also built for the Scottish fleet and this led to all the Scottish steam drifters being phased out a number of years in advance of those in English ownership. In 1952, the average earnings of a steam drifter ranged from the highest of £7300 to the lowest of £1700, and as the years passed, coal became more expensive and earnings generally became unpredictable. Some farsighted English owners still operating steam drifters did decide that diesel powered vessels were the way forward, and a few purchased Admiralty MFVs whilst others invested heavily in completely new vessels. In 1949, a major change in drifter design was unveiled when the first of a new generation of drifters appeared. The Ruston diesel engine powered *Frederick Spashett* was built by Richards Ironworks (Yard No. 388) at Lowestoft in 1949.

LT138 *Frederick Spashett*
(MWC)

She was built for Pevensey Castle Ltd., one of the great many subsidiaries of the long standing Lowestoft fishing vessel owners Small & Co. which was headed by Major D. F. (Tony) Cartwright MC, MBE, TD. The vessel was named in honour of his grandfather, a Mayor of Lowestoft and a leading figure in the fishing industry and the business life of the town of Lowestoft. *Frederick Spashett* proved to be a most pleasing and well laid out design that soon became respected throughout the British herring industry. Following on from the success of this vessel, Small & Co. went on to become the owners of a fleet of efficient robust modern drifters able to undertake trawling if required. As the fortunes of the herring fishing declined sharply in the 1960s, Small & Co. remained very active in the fishing industry by investing heavily in a fleet of quality built large diesel side and stern trawlers, many of which later went on to work as support vessels in the offshore oil and gas industry and are still at work in 2006 under different ownership. Prior to the building of *Frederick Spashett*, a few other diesel powered drifters had been built at Lowestoft such as the *Veracity* in 1926, the drifter/trawler *J. A. P.* in 1931, and the drifter/trawlers *Boston Spitfire* and *Boston Mosquito* in 1947. Following the very successful *Frederick Spashett*, in the 1950s and 1960s many more versatile drifter/trawlers were built. Some of these were for the leading Yarmouth drifter and trawler owner, Bloomfields Ltd., a typical example being the *Ocean Crest*, built by Richards in 1956. The last English drifter/trawlers to enter service included *Valiant*

LT277 *Valiant Star*
(MWC)

Star built by Richards in 1959 for Star Drift Fishing Co. Ltd., the *Boston Hornet*, built in 1960 at Brightlingsea for Boston Deep Sea Fisheries Ltd. and *Suffolk Warrior* (See Page 95).
During 1957, a new type of drifter/trawler appeared at Yarmouth when two large vessels of Polish origin arrived and started herring fishing with the conventional drifters. These two became YH370 *Autumn Sun* and YH372 *Autumn Star*, and were considered very

modern with better facilities and equipment than many British built drifters. The first landing by one of these vessels was on 28th September, when *Autumn Star* landed 16 crans of herring. Later these vessels discharged barrels of herring, cured at sea by their crews, at Yarmouth.

The steam drifter KY21 *Coriedalis* at Lowestoft (*MWC*)

A sign of rapidly changing times in the herring industry came in 1956, when amongst the large number of Scottish motor drifters at Yarmouth, there was just one Scottish steam drifter, a much different scene from when the river there was crowded with hundreds of these much admired craft. Built as an Admiralty standard drifter in 1918 at Aberdeen, KY21 *Coriedalis*, was still making good landings such as that on 20th October when she put ashore 160 crans at Yarmouth.

The following year her skipper, James Muir, brought a new diesel powered drifter, KY124 *Silver Chord* to Yarmouth and went on to win the Prunier Trophy (See Page 88). With no Scottish steam drifters at Yarmouth for the autumn fishing in 1957, steam power there was represented by the seven remaining local drifters made up of KY322 *Wilson Line*, YH33 *Noontide*, YH78 *Rosebay*, YH92 *Achievable*, YH105 *Wydale*, YH126 *Young Cliff* and YH278 *Harry Eastick*. A number of steam drifters owned by Lowestoft and Yarmouth owners were converted to diesel power during the 1950s although some of these did very little herring fishing once converted, their owners deciding that trawling was more profitable and with consistent returns. One of these was the *Wilson Line,* for many years owned by Chas V. Eastick of Gorleston. She carried the Scottish port letters and fishing number KY322 for the majority of her life, but in her last years carried the port letters and fishing number YH105, previously seen on a number of sold or scrapped Eastick owned vessels. *Wilson Line* was sold in 1973 to new local owners who after two years sold the vessel to new owners in Greece.

The very last East Anglian steam drifter, the Yarmouth drifter *Wydale*, left for the breakers yard in Holland on 29th October 1961. She held the distinction of being the last steam drifter to operate from any United Kingdom port. Lowestoft's last steam drifter, *Lizzie West*, had been taken out of service a few weeks earlier in the same year, both of these were of wood construction and owned by members of the Eastick family. The last Lowestoft steel built steam drifter was the former Scottish registered *Prime,* owned by the well known Lowestoft drifter owner Mr. J. J. Colby. She was also sold for scrapping in 1961.

The last Yarmouth herring drifters, all relatively modern diesel vessels were purchased by Small & Co. (Lowestoft) Ltd. in 1963 and saw a few more years use working from Lowestoft.

With rapidly declining herring stocks, the Scottish drifters, for so long the mainstay of the East Anglian fishery became fewer and fewer until the point was reached when it just was not an economic proposition for any number of these vessels to come this far south. Whether they were sail, steam or motor powered, Scottish drifters were always well cared for, very smart in appearance and a great credit to the owners, skippers and crews.

By November 1967, only two drifters from the once large Small & Co. fleet were still fishing. Considered at the time the worst herring season ever, only a few worthwhile catches were made. The highlights of the season included the landing on 13th November by the *Norfolk Yeoman* under Skipper George Meen when she landed 125 crans, and on the 14th November when the former Yarmouth drifter *Ocean Surf* under Skipper Donald Smith landed 126 crans of fresh herring and 40 of iced. Some of these herring were in nets handed over by the *Norfolk Yeoman* the previous day. The 14th November also saw the *Wisemans,* under Skipper Arthur Utting, land 57 crans that sold for around £900. On 5th December, *Norfolk Yeoman* landed just 3 crans and *Ocean Surf* landed 10 crans. The fish made £25 to £26 a cran and became the very last landings by any of the Small & Co. drifters. At Lowestoft only 20 drifters took part in the 1967 herring season, 17 Scottish drifters and three English. The English drifters landed 3,267 crans worth £36,614 and the 17 Scottish vessels landed 2,518 crans worth £22,466. During the previous herring season, 26 drifters landed 15,152 crans worth £127,492.

Following this disastrous season, some of the drifters of the Small & Co. fleet were converted for trawling and others undertook support work for the booming offshore oil and gas industry before being sold for further use as fishing vessels in Scotland or overseas, whilst one, the *Ocean Crest*, became a research vessel.

The 1968 season saw only one Lowestoft drifter, the James J. Colby owned LT382 *Wisemans*, still seeking the shoals during October. Only a few landings of small quantities of fish were made and by the end of December that year she had finished fishing, was laid up, and advertised for sale.

Historically, by far the greatest majority of drifters participating in the East Anglian herring fishery were Scottish owned, and it was perhaps ironic that the very last East Anglian herring drifter was previously a Scottish vessel.

The very last Scottish drifters appeared in 1970 when FR59 *Golden Gain* and FR106 *Girl Marlene* came south. Two Peterhead pair trawlers visited Yarmouth in 1971 and four arrived at Lowestoft in 1973 seeking the elusive herring.

Only a few survivors of the hundreds of sail, steam and diesel powered drifters built remain to remind us, and future generations, of a past major East Anglian annual event. Today the surviving vessels are either preserved heritage vessels such as the Scottish vessel *Reaper*, or those converted for other uses. Examples of these being the diesel powered *Young Elizabeth, Scotch Queen,* and the *Ocean Dawn.* The 1930 built steam Yarmouth drifter/trawler *Lydia Eva*, is preserved and awaits major restoration at Lowestoft. She was owned by Harry Eastick, and had a very short working life as a herring drifter.

The *Wisemans* became the very last English drifter to work from Lowestoft or Yarmouth when she finished fishing on 21st November 1968. For her last landing, after staying on the fishing grounds for 3 nights, she made just £2.10s. 0d (£2.50p). A former Admiralty 75 ft. MFV, she was built at the George Forbes shipyard at Peterhead in 1943, and before being purchased by Lowestoft owner James J. Colby was owned by the Wiseman family of Gardenstown, and bore the port letters and fishing number BF154. In 1968, *Wisemans* was sold by Mr. Colby to new owners in Ireland and given the Irish port letters and fishing number W38. Ironically, in 1961, Mr. Colby had been the owner of *Prime*, the last working steel steam drifter. *Wisemans* sank 24 miles off County Louth, Eire on 11th March 1984. She is seen here leaving Yarmouth after landing herring there. *(MWC)*

A Selection of Scottish Registered Drifters at Yarmouth, Lowestoft and Southwold

With little wind, and the crew using sweeps to propel the vessel, a Methil registered sailing drifter leaves Lowestoft Harbour at the end of the 19th century. Banff and Kirkcaldy registered vessels wait to follow out through the pier heads. (*MWC*)

An assortment of Scottish sailing and steam drifters, together with local trawlers and drifters leave Lowestoft in the early 1900s. Close examination shows thirty nine fishing vessels on this print, only two of which are steam powered. (*MWC*)

With other ports full to capacity, Southwold was able to offer space for the Scottish fisher girls to work, full facilities for the Scottish drifters and a harbour capable of taking cargo ships used for the export of cured herring. This is the harbour at Southwold in 1908. The nearest steam drifter is the 1903 built BF1263 *Handy*, whose owner lived in Buckie. (*DMC*)

Moored near the Town Hall at Yarmouth in the early 1900s and very convenient for the crews to visit shops and other town centre facilities, these Fraserburgh, Wick and Banff drifters would be a major tourist attraction today, but when this scene was recorded it was just an ordinary event. (*MWC*)

A one time familiar scene at Gorleston as Scottish steam drifters follow Kirkcaldy and Banff registered sailing drifters being towed out of Yarmouth harbour. (*MWC*)

An assortment of Scottish steam drifters at Yarmouth with Aberdeen, Banff, Buckie and Kirkcaldy registered vessels present. Two of the vessels with Aberdeen port letters are A380 *Glentana* and the other A386 *Glenshee*, both belonging to the Steam Herring Fleet Ltd., Aberdeen. The Kirkcaldy registered vessel on the left is KY218 *Pride o' Fife*, built in 1907 at Portgordon and owned by J. Watson, Cellardyke. (*MWC*)

A busy scene at Southwold as drifters land herring at a time when landings at the three ports were approaching the highest level ever recorded. The nearest steam drifter is the Inverness registered INS286 *Violet* and next to her the Banff registered BF1277 *Hyssop*. The *Violet* was built in 1907 at Porthleven and the *Hyssop* in 1903 at Whiteinch. (*DMC*)

Scottish motor drifters pack the quayside at Yarmouth in the 1950s as they land their catches. As always, the Scottish vessels are seen to be well maintained and a great credit to their owners and crew. (*MWC*)

In October 1957, a review of the herring fishing fleet took place off Yarmouth. The salute was taken by Commander in Chief, Nore, Admiral Sir Frederick Parham on HMS *Wave*. Other vessels taking part in the review included HMS *Lennox* and HMS *Bramble*. A Polish fishery training ship was also present. This is the view from HMS *Lennox* as over 150 drifters, mainly Scottish, passed by. Each section was to be led by the 1956 Prunier Herring Trophy winners, *Stephens* leading the Yarmouth section and *Silver Crest*, the Lowestoft section. However, due to a delay incurred whilst landing a sizable catch at Lowestoft, *Silver Crest* was unable to participate and her place was taken by LT235 *Silver Seas*. All three warships were "Algerine" Class ocean minesweepers attached to the fishery protection squadron. (*MWC*)

Scottish drifters dressed overall at Yarmouth in 1957 in preparation for the review of the fishing fleet in which some longshore boats also took part. During the review, as each drifter passed HMS *Wave,* the engines were slowed and four fishermen in oilskins stood on each foredeck with one saluting the Admiral. The review was the first event of the revived East Anglian Fair, and was described as a "fine spectacle" in what had been a meagre herring season. *(MWC)*

A342 *Indian Summer* entering Lowestoft.
Built in 1918 at Aberdeen.
(*MWC*)

BF484 *Harvest Gleaner* leaving Lowestoft.
Built in 1918 at Oulton Broad.
(*MWC*)

For many years drifters leaving port together during the herring season was considered a normal occurrence at both Lowestoft and Yarmouth and could be witnessed well into the late 1950s. The nearest vessel of the thirteen steam drifters seen here leaving Lowestoft is BF148 *J. & M. Main,* owned by Mr. W. Donaldson of Portknockie. She was built in 1913 at Yarmouth. *(MWC)*

BF1122 *Magnet* leaving Yarmouth.
Built in 1903 at Yarmouth.
(*MWC*)

BK63 *Enterprising* leaving Yarmouth.
Built in 1914 at Findochty.
(*MWC*)

Lowestoft shipbuilder John Chambers was well known for building quality steam drifters and built many for Scottish and English owners. Completed at the shipyard in 1904, BF1492 *Star of Hope* was owned A. Watt of Banff and was a typical example of an early steam drifter. She is is seen here at Lowestoft. *(MWC)*

BK148 *Helen Ann* entering Lowestoft. Built in 1915 at Buckie.
(MWC)

BCK100 *Maggie Gault* entering Yarmouth. Built in 1910 at Aberdeen.
(MWC)

BCK355 *Obtain* entering Lowestoft. Built in 1917 at Findochty.
(MWC)

FR240 *M. A. West* entering Lowestoft. Built in 1919 at Oulton Broad.
(MWC)

A classic view of FR487 *Sunbeam* leaving Lowestoft in the early 1960s for the herring grounds. This fine and superbly maintained craft was in the ownership of the Duthie family of Fraserburgh at the time. Only in the final years of the fishery were drifters equipped with radar, seen here on the *Sunbeam*. (*MWC*)

FR187 *Dewy Rose* leaving Lowestoft.
Built in 1915 at Aberdeen.
(*MWC*)

INS365 *Drainie* entering Yarmouth.
Built in 1918 at Fraserburgh.
(*MWC*)

INS137 *Mary Flett* leaving Lowestoft.
Built in 1919 at Oulton Broad.
(MWC)

KY173 *Fair Haven* leaving Yarmouth.
Built in 1918 at Oulton Broad.
(MWC)

KY185 *Agnes Gardner* entering Yarmouth.
Built 1920 at Hook.
(MWC)

LH3 *Resolute* entering Yarmouth.
Built in 1886 at Leith,
(MWC)

It is a bright dry morning at Gorleston as PD358 *Anchor of Hope* passes the lifeboat boathouses and makes her way up river with the crew tidying the drifter up, and preparing to land the catch. Owned by Adam M. Stewart and partners of Peterhead, the *Anchor of Hope* was built in 1944 at St. Monance.

LH273 *Craighall* entering Lowestoft.
Built in 1920 at Queensferry.
(*MWC*)

LK173 *Gossa Water* entering Lowestoft.
Built in 1918 at Lowestoft.
(*MWC*)

LK374 *Lord Curzon* entering Lowestoft. Built in 1917 at Oulton Broad.
(MWC)

PD96 *Hope* leaving Lowestoft.Built in 1906 at Aberdeen.
(MWC)

PD243 *Trust* leaving Yarmouth. Built in 1918 at Aberdeen.
(MWC)

SY397 *Surprise* entering Yarmouth. Built in 1902 at Lowestoft.
(MWC)

WK177 *Pilot Us* entering Lowestoft. Built in 1918 at Banff.
(*MWC*)

WK254 *Bon Avenir* at Yarmouth. Built in 1910 at Lowestoft.
(*MWC*)

BF180 *Mary Jane* leaving Lowestoft. Built in 1930 at Macduff.
(*MWC*)

BF363 *Helen West* leaving Lowestoft. Built 1937 at Sandhaven.
(*MWC*)

The wooden Scottish steam drifter BF189 *Monitor* was built by Fellows & Co. at Yarmouth in 1906. She was one of those built at the yard that had a raised quarter deck by about 8 inches, to give more headroom in the aft cabin. Of the two prints on this page, the larger image was recorded on 20th April 1906 and the other about 3 weeks later. The first owners of *Monitor* were A. Smith, Ianstown and partners. (*Both MWC*)

BCK152 *Girl Helen* entering Yarmouth. Built in 1934 at Buckie.
(*MWC*)

BCK114 *Three Bells* entering Lowestoft. Built in 1937 at Sandhaven.
(*MWC*)

BK250 *Isa Wilson* entering Lowestoft. Built in 1907 at Cockenzie.
(*MWC*)

BK276 *Cissie* leaving Lowestoft. Built in 1928 at Eyemouth.
(*MWC*)

FR965 *Comfort* entering Lowestoft. Built in 1936 at Fraserburgh. War loss at Dunkirk in May1940 *(MWC)*

FR965 *Rotche* leaving Lowestoft. Built in 1941 at Sandhaven. *(MWC)*

INS133 *Narinia* leaving Yarmouth. Built in 1934 at Buckie. *(MWC)*

KY38 *Elspeth Smith* entering Yarmouth. Built in 1904 at St. Monance. *(MWC)*

KY40 *Gleanaway* entering Yarmouth. Built in 1930 at Sandhaven. *(MWC)*

LK64 *Ocean Reaper* entering Lowestoft. Built in 1944 at St. Monance. *(MWC)*

ML38 *Gowan* entering Lowestoft. Built in 1903 at Peterhead. *(MWC)*

PD160 *Caledonia* leaving Yarmouth. Built in 1933 at Macduff. Lost off West Coast in 1952 *(MWC)*

With most of the visiting drifter fleet coming from other Scottish ports, PD267 *Fertility* was one of the few regular Peterhead drifters to visit Lowestoft annually in the 1950s. Owned by James G. Hay and partners of Peterhead, the green hulled drifter is seen here approaching the pier heads at the port. (*MWC*)

PD326 *Fertile Vale* at Yarmouth. Built in 1954 at Peterhead. (*MWC*)

Herrings come ashore in a modern aluminium trunk from the green hulled Prunier Herring Trophy record holder PD417 *Fruitful Bough*. Built in 1948 at Peterhead, she became a total loss after running ashore in 1961. (*MWC*)

The Prunier Herring Trophy 1936-66

The Prunier Herring Trophy competition was held from 1936 until 1966 during the East Anglian autumn herring fishery. Vessels eligible to enter were the large number of Scottish and English herring drifters participating in the fishery and operating from the ports of Great Yarmouth and Lowestoft. The Trophy was not awarded between 1940 and 1945, nor in 1965, when no claims were submitted to the competition committee.

It should not be confused with another Prunier Trophy that was associated with the catering industry.

The idea of an award was that of Madame Simone Prunier, the grand daughter of Alfred Prunier who founded the great Paris restaurant, Maison Prunier, in 1872. When Alfred died at the age of 49, the running of the restaurant passed to Emile Alfred Prunier, the youngest of Alfred's three children. Emile married in 1900, but sadly his wife was taken suddenly ill in May 1901 and died. In October 1902, Emile remarried and in 1903, Simone was born. From an early age, Simone was to help her father in the running of the business and in 1923, she married Jean Barnagaud, one of her father's most promising executives. Upon the death of her father, Madame Simone Prunier was left in sole charge of the business at the age of 22, the very same age at which her father had taken over the running of the restaurant from his father in 1898.
Madame Prunier set about further establishing the restaurant as one of best-known and highly rated in Paris and in 1935, the business was further expanded when a new Prunier's was opened in St. James's Street, London. Following the successful launch of this new venture, Madame Prunier and her husband settled in London. In a discussion with business colleagues at a lunch following the opening of the new restaurant, Madame Prunier was made aware of the parlous state that the British herring industry was in and was surprised to be told that the British cared little for the herring with fewer being eaten each year by the public who did not see the herring in the same light as some gourmets, who described it as the "King of Fish" and having a flavour as delicious and as individual as trout. The many different ways that the herring could be prepared and presented at meal times did little to increase the sales of the fish. A number of possible reasons for the increasing unpopularity of the herring were discussed at the lunch and these included the fact that the fish was considered "cheap and common" by many and that the boniness of it made it difficult for some people to eat and enjoy. Another reason considered was that the public appeared to be increasingly attracted to white fish in preference to the herring with vast quantities of white fish being consumed in "Fish and Chips" and other meals.

Whatever the reasons were for the lack of consumers, the result was that many hundreds of thousands of herring were being thrown back into the sea unwanted, or were being reduced to fish meal for use in animal feed or fertiliser after being landed at the herring ports and having being sold off at a very low price. Unhappy with this situation, Madame Prunier decided to seek ways in which she could help the industry by stimulating interest in the herring and promoting sales in both the home and export markets. Part of her plan was to increase public awareness of the fact that the East Anglian herring fishery produced the very finest type of herrings, full of spawn and of high nutritive value and to this end she needed something significant that would attract the attention of readers of the local and national newspapers, and listeners to the wireless. After a great deal of thought, followed by discussions with those in the trade, she made a generous and unique gesture when deciding to set up an annual competition that would conclude with an award being presented to the skipper and crew landing the largest single catch of herring between early October and the end of November at the ports of Great Yarmouth or Lowestoft.

The new venture was strongly supported by the herring fishing community on the East Coast, the Ministry of Agriculture and Fisheries, the Scottish Herring Catchers Association and the English Herring Catchers Association. In addition, Mr. George Atkinson, the Fisheries Inspector at Lowestoft and later to become the Chairman of the Herring Industries Board, provided valuable assistance. After much deliberation, it was decided that the competition would be known as the "Prunier Herring Trophy".

To enable the competition to be run during the forthcoming 1936 autumn herring fishery, an organising committee with their headquarters in Lowestoft was quickly arranged and set about formulating the rules of the competition. A distinguished sculptor, Charles Sykes was commissioned to create a suitable trophy in Purbeck marble and this resulted in a most suitable design featuring a hand rising from a breaking wave and grasping a herring. Details of the new competition were released on 20th July 1936 and for the first year, the competition ran from 5th October to 28th November. A similar period was used during future years. The drifter that hauled and landed the largest single catch of herring in one night's fishing would be declared the winner and the drifter landing the second largest catch would be the runner up. However, if the winner was an English drifter, the runner up would have to be a Scottish vessel, or vice versa. When submitting a claim for the trophy, documentation would have to be presented to the committee within 48 hours of the landing, duly signed by the salesman and certified correct by an officer from the Ministry of Agriculture and Fisheries. Details of each year's winning catch, together with the Skipper's and drifter's name would be engraved on a brass plaque at the base of the Trophy. The Trophy and a cash prize of £25 would be presented at a ceremonial luncheon organised at Prunier's Restaurant in St. James's, where a Guest of Honour would make the presentations. Also at the ceremony, a weather vane with the year on it would be presented to the winning skipper to be fixed to the drifter's fore or mizzen mast. A cash prize of £25 was presented to the runner up. A number of trips, such as to the zoo, were also laid on for the crew whilst in London. In later years, the winning skipper received a silver cigarette case and each member of his crew was given a silver ashtray. Those attending the ceremony would travel to London at Madame Prunier's expense. The presentation ceremony was not always held in London and was occasionally held locally, usually at the Great Yarmouth or Lowestoft Town Halls, or a hotel. In later years, it was always held locally.

Whilst not directly associated with the Prunier Herring Trophy competition, in a broadcast following the B.B.C. Fishing News Bulletin on 24th September 1958, Sir Frederick Bell, O.B.E., M.C., Chairman of the Herring Industry Board, announced that the Board was to run a series of competitions for herring fishermen during the forthcoming East Anglian season. This new initiative consisted of six weekly contests carrying prize money amounting in all to more than £2,000. The Board would award five prizes each week for six weeks from Monday 13th October with drifters that fished actively from Great Yarmouth or Lowestoft from the starting date to 22nd November being eligible to enter. The competition would be in two sections, Scottish and English, with the prizes going to the vessels whose herring landings in any one week at Great Yarmouth or Lowestoft realised the highest value at auction. Each week during the competition period, a £100 cash payment would be made to the English drifter grossing the largest sum plus a runner up payment of £50 for the second highest earning English vessel. Because of the far larger number of Scottish vessels participating in the fishery, the prizes would be three weekly payments of £100, £75 and £50 for the first, second and third highest earners each week in this section.

A major change in the Prunier Herring Trophy competition occurred later the same month, when on the 29th September 1958, a press release from Madame Prunier's office announced that she had decided to offer the Prunier Herring Trophy to the Herring Industry Board in order that it should henceforth be awarded by the Board. The Prunier Herring Trophy Competition would no longer be organised by Madame Prunier. In agreement with the Adjudication Committee, Madame Prunier felt that, after the consecration of this competition by the presentation of the Trophy on its 21st anniversary in 1957 by the Duke of Edinburgh, her aim had been achieved, and that her efforts for the fishing industry should now be taken over by an official body. In conclusion, the press release stated that Madame Prunier wished to thank the many friends who, during the past 21 years, had helped her in her work on behalf of British fishermen, in whose welfare she would continue to take the most lively interest.
On 22nd November 1958, Madame Prunier officially handed over the Trophy to the Herring Industry Board at a brief ceremony in the Town Hall at Great Yarmouth.

During the last full year in which the Trophy was awarded by Madame Prunier, the organising committee included Sir Robert (later Lord) Boothby, M.P. for East Aberdeen, Edward Evans, M.P. for Lowestoft, Anthony Fell, M.P. for Yarmouth, and W. Smith Duthie, M.P. for Banff, as well as leading figures in the herring industry. The guests of honour at the presentation ceremonies had included Lady Diana Cooper, Viscount Simon, General Sir Ian Hamilton, Sir Frederick Bell, Chairman of the Herring Industry

Board, Sir Alan Herbert, Admiral Sir Charles Lamb, then Second Sea Lord, the Rt. Hon. Alan Lennox-Boyd, secretary of State for the Colonies, and in 1957, H. R. H. Prince Philip, Duke of Edinburgh.

It became obvious that there had been a substantial decline in the amount of fish being caught during the time that the competition had been run, leading to fewer drifters taking part. The 1966 herring season became the last occasion that the competition was held, with the final drifter to win the Prunier Herring Trophy being the 1946 built FR346 *Tea Rose*.

The Trophy was later placed on permanent loan by the Herring Industry Board to the Port of Lowestoft Research Society and subsequently became an exhibit in the Lowestoft Maritime Museum where it can be seen today. This splendid and unique cottage museum, which records so much of the local herring fishery, is located in the Sparrows Nest Park in Lowestoft.

Constituted on 15th March 1935, the Herring Industry Board was abolished in 1981 when it amalgamated with the Sea Fish Industry Authority, to which all its liabilities were transferred.

PD417 *Fruitful Bough*
The drifter that landed the largest ever catch during the competition for the Prunier Herring Trophy 1936-66.
(MWC)

Prunier Herring Trophy 1936-66
THE WINNING SKIPPERS

1936	Joseph Mair
1937	David Knights
1938	William Bowles
1939	Fred Darkins
1940	No competition
1941	No competition
1942	No competition
1943	No competition
1944	No competition
1945	No competition
1946	Walter Rudd
1947	H. G. Meen
1948	Arthur Keable
1949	Stanley Turrell
1950	Alfred Brown
1951	George Forman
1952	Ernest Thompson
1953	Peter Forman
1954	Robert Williamson
1955	George Duncan
1956	Fred Stephens
1956	Arthur Utting
1957	James Muir
1958	Ernest Thompson
1959	George Draper
1960	James Cardno
1961	Leo Borrett
1962	Stanley Hewitt
1963	Ritson Sims
1964	Ernest Fiske
1965	No claims submitted
1966	Charles Duthie

Note
Joint Winners in 1956

Winning Drifters and the Runners Up

Year	Winning Drifter / Runner Up	Crans	Port
1936	BF592 *Boy Andrew*	231	Yarmouth
	YH217 *Frons Olivae*	224¼	Yarmouth
1937	LT47 *Peace Wave*	271	Lowestoft
	BK260 *Excel III*	249½	Yarmouth
1938	LT167 *Hosanna*	238	Lowestoft
	FR124 *Allochy*	196¾	Yarmouth
1939	LT89 *Present Friends*	194½	Lowestoft
	BCK453 *Attain*	174¾	Yarmouth
1946	YH63 *Romany Rose*	246¾	Yarmouth
	PD598 *Tansy*	229¼	Yarmouth
1947	LT178 *Patria*	253	Lowestoft
	See Note 1		
1948	LT371 *Dauntless Star*	267¼	Lowestoft
	KY322 *Wilson Line*	201	Lowestoft
1949	LT276 *Herring Searcher*	253¾	Lowestoft
	FR74 *Breme*	231¼	Yarmouth
1950	YH105 *Wydale*	250¼	Yarmouth
	PD367 *Fumerole*	237¾	Yarmouth
1951	PD218 *Star of Bethlehem*	303½	Yarmouth
	LT152 *Thrifty*	290	Lowestoft
1952	LT20 *Lord Hood*	314¾	Lowestoft
	PD239 *Vernal*	206¼	Yarmouth
1953	PD417 *Fruitful Bough*	323½	Yarmouth
	YH29 *Ocean Lifebuoy*	301¼	Yarmouth
1954	LK509 *Jessie Sinclair*	272	Lowestoft
	KY322 *Wilson Line*	270	Yarmouth
	See Note 2		

Winning Drifters and the Runners Up

Year	Winning Drifter / Runner Up	Crans	Port
1955	PD234 *Morning Star*	210¾	Yarmouth
	LT46 *Silver Crest*	208½	Lowestoft
1956	FR156 *Stephens* (Joint Winner)	215	Yarmouth
	LT46 *Silver Crest* (Joint Winner)	215	Lowestoft
1957	KY124 *Silver Chord*	212⅓	Yarmouth
	YH78 *Rosebay*	175	Yarmouth
1958	LT156 *St. Luke*	162¾	Lowestoft
	See Note 3		
1959	LT367 *Dauntless Star*	189½	Lowestoft
1960	FR178 *Silver Harvest*	187	Yarmouth
1961	LT61 *Dick Whittington*	274½	Lowestoft
1962	YH61 *Ocean Starlight*	294⅓	Yarmouth
1963	LT137 *Norfolk Yeoman*	186½	Lowestoft
1964	LT671 *Suffolk Warrior*	276½	Yarmouth
1965	See Note 4		
1966	FR346 *Tea Rose*	128⅔	Yarmouth

Notes

1 No claims were submitted for the position of runner up in 1947.

2 KY322 *Wilson Line* was eligible for runner up in 1954 since although Scottish registered, she was English owned.

3 The rules were altered whereby there was no runner up after the 1957 competition.

4 No claims were submitted during the 1965 season.

In 1938, the steam drifter/trawler LT167 *Hosanna* won the Prunier Herring Trophy with 238 crans. Her crew are seen here at Lowestoft, after winning the Trophy. (*MWC*)

The 1950 season saw Skipper Alfred Brown in the Yarmouth steam drifter YH105 *Wydale* win the Trophy. Skipper Brown is seen here at the presentation receiving the winners weather vane for mounting on top of the mizzenmast of *Wydale*.
This fine steam drifter was destined to become the last British working steam drifter and in 1961 when she was sold for breaking up, the weather vane was presented to the local maritime museum at Yarmouth. (*MWC*)

The drifter LT20 *Lord Hood* won the competition in 1952, and her Skipper Ernest Thompson is seen here with the Prunier Herring Trophy on the left, the dated weather vane for mounting on top of the drifter's mizzen mast , and a pair of binoculars for Skipper Thompson. The presentation was held at the Royal Hotel in Lowestoft. (*LESMS*)

The crew of the motor drifter PD417 *Fruitful Bough* at the presentation at the Queens Hotel, Yarmouth in 1953 after winning the competition that year with a landing of 323½ crans. At the presentation Skipper Peter Forman said in some cases the skipper got "too much honour" and that the crew often deserved more credit that they got. He also commented on the drifter's echo sounder and fish finder, stating that "it was safe to say that without it, they would never have got the catch". (*LESMS*)

In 1954, the Shetland drifter LK509 *Jessie Sinclair* won the competition with a landing of 272 crans. Skipper Robert Williamson and his crew travelled to London for the presentation and are seen here with Madame Prunier at the ceremony. On the table in front of the Trophy are binoculars for the Skipper and the presentation cake. (*LESMS*)

Skipper Ritson Sims, in the white pullover, with the crew of LT137 *Norfolk Yeoman* at Lowestoft in November 1963 after the announcement that they had won the competition that year. (*MWC*)

Top Right-In 1956, there were joint winners of the Prunier Herring Trophy competition and it was also the last occasion that a steam drifter was a winner. The steam drifter was LT46 *Silver Crest* and her crew are seen here at the presentation in London with Madame Prunier. The other joint winner was the Scottish drifter FR156 *Stephens*. (*LESMS*)

Bottom Left-The winning drifter in 1961 was LT61 *Dick Whittington* under Skipper Leo Borrett. The presentation that year was held at the Town Hall in Lowestoft where Skipper Borrett is seen receiving the Trophy from the Mayor of Lowestoft, Mr. Frank Jones. (*LESMS*)

Bottom Right-In 1962, it was the turn of Yarmouth to win the Trophy when YH61 *Ocean Starlight* under Skipper Stanley Hewitt was the winner. The Mayor of Yarmouth, Mr. J. Birchenall, is seen here presenting Skipper Hewitt with the mast head weather vane.

The 1964 winning drifter was LT671 *Suffolk Warrior* under Skipper Ernest "Jumbo" Fiske. Awarded the MBE in 1970 for services to the British fishing industry, Skipper Fiske is seen here holding the envelope containing the official notification of the award from Buckingham Palace. *(MWC)*

A fine study recorded in 1955 in the wheelhouse of the drifter PD234 *Morning Star* of Skipper George Duncan and the Kelvin Hughes echo sounder, used to locate the herring that made up the Prunier Trophy winning catch that year. *(LESMS)*

The 1936 Winning Drifter

BF592 Boy Andrew - 231 crans

The first winner of the Prunier Herring Trophy competition was built in 1918 at the shipyard of J. Lewis & Sons Ltd., Aberdeen as the Admiralty standard steel drifter HMD *Sunburst* (Admiralty No. 3924). In 1921, HMD *Sunburst* was sold by the Admiralty for use as a fishing vessel and became the Portsoy steam drifter BF592 *Boy Andrew*. She landed the winning catch at Yarmouth on 5th November 1936. In 1940 *Boy Andrew* was requisitioned for naval duties and undertook auxiliary patrol work. She was lost on 9th November 1941 following a collision with the steamship *St. Rognvald* in the Firth of Forth. The 1936 season was one of abundance of herring and the Herring Industry Board imposed restrictions on the fishing to prevent the markets becoming saturated. These restrictions included a limit on the number of nets to be used by skippers, the length of the nets used and, at selected times, drifters being prevented from leaving harbour. With 624 drifters at Yarmouth and many more at Lowestoft, the season was one of consistent good landings and catches of over 100 crans were common. PD81 *Marigold*, LT1296 *Landbreeze*, YH81 *Craiglea* and YH217 *Frons Olivae* all landed catches of 200 crans or over during the season which was marred by the loss of PD77 *Olive Branch*. She capsized in a storm near the Corton light vessel, with the loss of all nine of her crew. The crew of a nearby drifter, PD178 *Young Dawn* saw the capsizing and said the *Olive Branch* was hit by a very heavy sea that threw her on her beam ends, and before she could right herself, another sea capsized her. Six of those lost were from the same family, Skipper William Cowie had his sons William junior, David and George, cousin Andrew Cowie and his son Andrew Junior with him. The *Olive Branch* was washed ashore the following day, grounding on an even keel, at Kessingland. Two other drifters, BF151 *Pitgaveney* and YH530 *Queen of the Fleet*, were caught in the same seas and suffered damage on that dreadful day, but no lives were lost. *(MWC)*

The 1937 Winning Drifter

LT47 Peace Wave - 271 crans

Herring were plentiful throughout the 1937 fishery with large quantities being landed by almost 800 drifters working out of Yarmouth and Lowestoft. Many vessels landed catches of over 200 crans, examples of these being INS101 *Moray Rose* and PD487 *North Briton* with 240 crans each, PD520 *Principal* and PD170 *Ephratah* with 250 crans each, YH89 *Lydia Eva* with 221 crans, LT201 *Quiet Waters* with $247\frac{3}{4}$ crans and BK260 *Excel III* with $249\frac{1}{2}$ crans. Generally, demand on the markets was high, the herring finding a ready market with the exporters needing vast quantities, although on some days the market became saturated and poor quality herring were dumped. Lowestoft's first winner in the competition, *Peace Wave,* landed her winning catch, caught on the Smith's Knoll grounds, at Lowestoft on 28th October. The crew had spent over 12 hours hauling in the nets, some of which were lost due to the weight of fish they contained. By 1937, 120 of those drifters involved in the fishery had been fitted with radio and 80 with fish finding echometers. The radio fitted to LT345 *Primevere* became essential in September when fishing on the Dowsing grounds, it allowed her to call for help after becoming swamped with herring and even more left in her nets. LT44 *Lord Suffolk* answered the call, and took over many of the nets. Both drifters headed for Yarmouth where despite many herring being lost into the sea, *Primevere* landed 215 crans and *Lord Suffolk* landed 73 crans. *Peace Wave* was built in 1922 by Cochrane & Sons Ltd., Selby as H477 *Telia*. After three years she was re-registered GY299. During March 1929, *Telia* moved to Lowestoft and later that year became LT47 *Peace Wave*. Her first Lowestoft owner was William J. Westgate, this later changed to A. Westgate and a few years after that, she was in the ownership of P.W. Watson & Sons. A steel hulled drifter/trawler, *Peace Wave* was initially fitted with a 20nhp compound engine built by the International Engine Works at Amherst, Canada. This was replaced with a $44\frac{1}{2}$nhp Richards triple expansion engine at Richards shipyard in Lowestoft after she came into local ownership. *Peace Wave* was sold for scrapping and left Lowestoft together with the drifter *Landbreeze* on 13th July 1955 for the breakers yard. (*MWC*)

LT167 Hosanna - 238 crans

The 1938 season again proved to be one of great abundance of herring in the southern North Sea and with a similar number of drifters taking part in the fishing, although some of the older Yarmouth vessels had been disposed of at auction. In the sale, YH667 *Boy Bob* and YH8 *Dusty Miller* made £100, YH129 *Helpmate* made £90, YH927 *Ma Freen*, YH610 *Nulli Secundus* and YH579 *Cheerio Lads* all made £50, YH866 *Girl Marjorie* made £40 and YH719 *Oakland* went for £35. Three of these vessels were towed to Rotterdam by the Bristol tug *Fairplay II* for breaking up. The Prunier Trophy competition was set to run from 11th October until 26th November. The Herring Industry Board again imposed restrictions on the owners and skippers of drifters on the quantity (six per crewman) and size of nets used, when drifters could leave port and constraints on the price paid for the fish. Markets during the middle of October were overloaded with herring on several occasions and an example of the restrictions regulating fish supply was that after the severe glut of 18th October, no drifters sailed from Yarmouth or Lowestoft the following day. Despite these measures, it was still quite common for many drifters to arrive at both ports with catches exceeding 100 crans and many over 200 crans. There was a slight decrease in the number of barrels of herring exported in 1938 with around 190,000 going to ports such as Riga, Gdynia, Memel and Danzig. The 1938 competition winner, *Hosanna,* was built by John Chambers Ltd., Oulton Broad in 1930 and was initially owned by Albert E. Beamish. She landed her winning catch, caught on the Smith's Knoll fishing grounds, at Lowestoft on 10th November. Requisitioned in late 1939, *Hosanna* was given the Admiralty No. FY950 and after conversion, assigned minesweeping duties. She was handed back to her owners in November 1944 and went on to have a long life being converted from steam to diesel propulsion at Richards shipyard in 1960. After conversion to diesel power, *Hosanna* spent many successful years as a trawler before being sold for scrapping in 1976 at Oulton Broad, very close to where she was built. *(MWC)*

The 1939 Winning Drifter

LT89 Present Friends -194½ crans

The 1939 herring season got under way in very difficult circumstances with Admiralty fishing restrictions in force, drifters being requisitioned for naval duties, permits required to fish and a government scheme controlling the price paid for herring. With six Lowestoft wooden hulled drifters leaving the port to work on a particularly dangerous naval mission to try to recover intact at least one German mine of the type being laid in the Thames Estuary, others were still herring fishing. Despite the requirements for drifters to undertake naval duties thus leaving a diminished number available for fishing, many continued to be disposed of. Although there had been plenty of herring to catch in past seasons, prices were quite often low with little money being made. The spring of 1939 saw YH331 *Bono*, YH972 *Young Sam*, YH711 *Harry and Leonard* and YH11 *Radiant Rose* sold to overseas buyers for breaking up. The competition ran for a restricted period from 31st October until 30th November with around only 200 drifters fishing from Yarmouth and Lowestoft. The winning drifter, *Present Friends*, was a wooden hulled vessel built in 1914 by S. Richards & Co. Ltd. at Lowestoft as Yard No. 194 for the joint ownership of Mr. W. J. Turrell and Mr. E. T. Capps. Her Skipper was Fred Darkins. She was requisitioned in July 1915 and served in the First World War after being assigned the Admiralty No. 1565. Armed with a 6pdr. anti aircraft gun, *Present Friends* joined many other drifters carrying out indicator net duties. After being sold to Claude Spriggs in 1946, her fishing days were over. She set sail for Australia but developed a leak in the English Channel and sank at Helford. *Present Friends* was raised and taken to Shoreham where she was broken up. (*MWC*)

The 1946 Winning Drifter

YH63 Romany Rose - 246¾ crans

Whilst no competition was held in 1945, a large number of drifters assembled at Yarmouth and Lowestoft for the annual autumn fishing but the Admiralty would not allow any herring fishing until mines in the areas favoured by the skippers had been dealt with. By 7th October 1945, landings had resumed with *Ocean Swell,* owned by Bloomfields of Great Yarmouth, making the first landing from the local grounds with a catch of 15 crans. *Romany Rose*, the 1946 competition winner was a wooden hulled drifter built at the John Chambers yard at Lowestoft in 1924 with her boiler and 29nhp triple expansion steam engine supplied by the Beccles firm of Elliot & Garrood. Her first owner was Walter Rudd of Winterton. She was registered on 8th September and ran sea trials on the 11th. On 26th November 1938 near the Newarp Light Vessel, *Romany Rose* lost her rudder and shipped a sea that caused considerable damage and partly flooded below decks. The Scottish steam drifter FR542 *Westhaven* towed her home to Yarmouth. With the end of the war, restrictions were put in place by the Herring Industry Board preventing fishing until October and restricting the number of nets used by skippers on the fishing grounds to six per crewman. However once fishing did commence, good catches were made with several in November of over 200 crans, examples of these being LT403 *Comrades* with 231 crans, YH47 *Ocean Dawn* with 210 crans and LT133 *Strive* with 245 crans. *Romany Rose* under Skipper Walter Rudd made her winning catch, which was landed at Yarmouth on 4th November, 30 miles north east of Cockle Gat. Her crew were hauling the 70 nets on board for 23 hours, and the fish was sold at auction for £950. On 4th November 1950, *Romany Rose* collided with Yarmouth Harbour North Pier and had to be put on the Spending Beach because of a fear of sinking. In 1955, this typical East Anglian drifter was broken up. (*MWC*)

The 1947 Winning Drifter

LT178 Patria - 253 crans

The herring were late in arriving on the Smith's Knoll fishing grounds and it was not until the second week in October that any significant catches were made there. The shoals were patchy and the erratic catches reflected this with drifters landing quantities varying from one box to over 200 crans on the same day. An example of this was 15th October, when good landings included that of YH189 *Ocean Pioneer* with 180 crans and 18th October when PD81 *Marigold* landed 150 crans, but on the 17th, 56 drifters could only discharge an average of 39 crans each. Late October and throughout November saw more consistent landings being made, a number of which were over 200 crans including those of YH73 *Rose Hilda* with 228 crans, INS382 *Brighton O' The North* with 240 crans, FR124 *Golden Harvest* with 220 crans, YH876 *Ocean Crest* with 240 crans and LT746 *Margaret Hide* with 245 crans. Late November saw PD175 *Lichen,* a former Yarmouth drifter, land 170 crans at her former home port. The fourth Lowestoft vessel to win the competition, *Patria*, was built in 1916 by Gebroeders Boot at Leiderdorp, Holland. She was a large steel drifter/trawler and one of a number purchased by Lowestoft owners in the 1930s from Dutch interests. *Patria* was powered by a 225bhp triple expansion steam engine built by Burgerhouts of Rotterdam. The winning catch was made on the Dowsing fishing grounds and *Patria,* under Skipper H. G. Meen, arrived at Lowestoft to land the fish on 18th October. Her owners, the Shoals Fishing Co. Ltd., sold her for scrapping in 1954 and she left Lowestoft for a breakers yard in Belgium. At the time the *Patria* was sold for scrapping, her owners were replacing many of their ageing steam powered vessels with new diesel powered drifter/trawlers all built at the Lowestoft shipyard of Richards Ironworks. (*MWC*)

The 1948 Winning Drifter

LT371 Dauntless Star - 267¼ crans

Launched in 1948 at the Cochrane & Sons Ltd. shipyard at Selby, the drifter/trawler *Dauntless Star* was one of two powerful and sturdy looking vessels built at the same yard. Her sister ship, launched as LT377 *Sunlit Waters*, also went on to be awarded the Trophy, when as LT367 *Dauntless Star* she became the 1959 winner.

Under Skipper Arthur Keable, LT371 *Dauntless Star* landed her winning catch at Lowestoft on 9th November where it sold at auction for £905. Whilst Lowestoft was gaining these new diesel powered drifter/trawlers, Bloomfields at Yarmouth took delivery of three steam powered vessels that became YH293 *Ocean Unity*, YH296 *Ocean Hunter* and YH344 *Ocean Sunbeam*. Launched between 1918 and 1920, all three were ordered by the Admiralty as standard drifters. The 1948 herring season was considered in the trade to have been one of the best ever, with a great abundance of fish, good prices, many landings of over 100 crans and over 200 crans not unusual. The Prunier Herring Trophy competition ran from 12th October until 23rd November and due to the consistent good landings early in the competition the position of leading drifter changed frequently as did that of the runner up. A number of drifters such as LT152 *Thrifty*, YH278 *Harry Eastick* and LT341 *Oceanbreeze*, were in the running for the Trophy, but none were to exceed the winning catch of the *Dauntless Star*. Owned by the Star Drift Fishing Co. Ltd., *Dauntless Star* had a brief working life from Lowestoft. She passed to Boston Deep Sea Fishing and Ice Co. Ltd. in 1951 and was sold the following year to Booth Fisheries Canadian Ltd. of Winnipeg and became the *Red Diamond IV* in 1954. In the above scene, *Dauntless Star* was recorded leaving Lowestoft in the early morning with other drifters for the fishing grounds, possibly on a Sunday morning in the autumn of 1949. At the top of her mizzen mast, the Prunier Herring Trophy winners weather vane can clearly be seen. *(GCC)*

The 1949 Winning Drifter

LT276 Herring Searcher - 253¾ crans

Early in the season good landings were made but bad weather in mid to late October affected the fishing and consequently landings dropped. The landings recorded at Yarmouth on 20th October demonstrate the situation well, with 160 drifters arriving there to discharge their catches that totalled 660 crans, an average of just over 4 crans per drifter. On 8th November 1949, the *Herring Searcher* under Skipper Stanley Turrell made the winning catch that was sold at Lowestoft for around £700. Built in 1914 by Livingstone & Cooper Ltd. at Hessle, *Herring Searcher* arrived at Yarmouth on 14th June 1914 under tow for the installation of her Crabtree 33nhp triple expansion engine. Carrying the port letters and fishing number YH51, she was initially owned by Mr. John T.C. Salmon but in 1928, passed into the ownership of Mr. Henry F. J. Eastick of Gorleston. During May 1939, she was sold into the ownership of B. Buchan of Coull and re-registered PD79. Within 5 years, *Herring Searcher* was on the move again and this time had her Peterhead registration replaced with that of BF19. Her return to English ownership was in January 1947, when the Shoals Fishing Co. Ltd. of Lowestoft purchased her and once again she was re-registered, this time to her final port fishing registration of LT276. In March 1915, *Herring Searcher* was requisitioned for naval work and given the Admiralty No. 1405. She was assigned net drifter duties and was eventually released back to her owner by the Admiralty in 1919. She was sold for scrapping and left Lowestoft on 9th June 1954. *(MWC)*

The 1950 Winning Drifter

YH105 Wydale - 250¼ crans

The wooden hulled *Wydale* held the distinction of being the very last steam drifter to fish from the United Kingdom. She sailed for the breakers yard in Zeeland on 29th October 1961 towing the Yarmouth pleasure steamer *Cobholm*. Built by John Chambers at Lowestoft in 1917, *Wydale* was named after an area between Pickering and Scarborough in East Yorkshire and was first registered at Whitby as WY225. After being purchased by Henry Frederick Eastick she gained the Yarmouth port letters and fishing number of YH105 and soon became known as a drifter for making good catches. On 23rd October 1950, she landed the winning catch at Yarmouth, but whilst on the fishing grounds, 60 crans of herring from the catch were passed over to the drifter *Harry Eastick* due to the amount of fish in the nets. Fishing was reasonable early in the season with good catches being made such as those by LT178 *Patria* with 190 crans and LT138 *Frederick Spashett* with 200 crans. The Scottish drifters did well in late October and throughout November with many landing catches of over 100 crans such as BF327 *Kooleen* with 140 crans. The season was considered satisfactory by the trade and 369 drifters had participated, of these just over 100 were English. *Wydale* was requisitioned in both World Wars for use on naval duties. During the First World War she was requisitioned in May 1918 and released the following year, and during the Second World War was requisitioned for use as an examination vessel in March 1940 and released back to her owner in March 1946. Many believe this superb example of an East Anglian built steam powered herring drifter should have been preserved instead of being broken up in an overseas breakers yard. (*MWC*)

The 1951 Winning Drifter

PD218 Star of Bethlehem - 303½ crans

A fine product of the Peterhead shipyard of George Forbes Ltd. in 1947, the *Star of Bethlehem* became the second Scottish drifter to win the competition when she landed her winning catch on 21st November at Yarmouth, the fish selling for around £910. For a number of years an annual visitor to East Anglia, her winning catch was made 19 miles east south east of the Leman buoy in very difficult conditions with the crew taking about 18 hours to haul the nets on board the drifter. For the majority of her life, this drifter was in the ownership of Mr. George Forman and partners and was sold in the early 1970s. Early October proved to be a disappointment with few good catches being made, but the second week saw an improvement with very worthwhile landings, many by Scottish drifters. By the third and fourth week in October several landings of over 100 crans had been made, and on 25th October, PD238 *Primrose* landed 214½ crans at Yarmouth and took the lead in the competition. The end of October and early November saw gales affecting fishing, but these seemed to stir the herring up and on 1st November, LT737 *Willing Boys* landed 219¼ crans and took the lead. This lead was short lived because there then followed a series of very good catches, some of which exceeded that of *Willing Boys*, including the 241 crans put ashore by LT495 *Lizzie West*, destined to become Lowestoft's last steam drifter in the 1960s. By the third week in November some of the Scottish drifters were heading for home, ironically around the same time as the *Star of Bethlehem* made her winning haul. *(MWC)*

The 1952 Winning Drifter

LT20 Lord Hood - 314 ¾ crans

Although landings of herring were very good initially, the 1952 herring fishery was noted for the seemingly endless series of gales that hampered the fishing. This year's Prunier Trophy competition was set to run from 14th October to 6th December, but until the middle of October bad weather was seriously affecting catches with erratic landings being made. The last week of October did see an improvement with some good catches being made, examples of these being YH138 *Animation* with 180 crans, YH264 *Ocean Spray,* YH167 *Ocean Sunlight,* PD239 *Vernal* and PD397 *Spes Melior* all with 200 crans each, LT1157 *Sarah Hide* with 235½ crans, PD239 *Vernal* with 206¼ crans and LT82 *Henrietta Spashett* with 249 crans. The gales returned again in November, but before that *Lord Hood* made her winning catch 17 miles north east of Smith's Knoll light vessel. Because she was so low in the water, as a precaution, *Lord Hood* was escorted part of the way back to Lowestoft by LT750 *Golden Miller,* both drifters sporting the colours of the well known Boston Group, complete with black and red funnels. Skipper Ernest Thompson brought *Lord Hood* into Lowestoft on 28th October where her arrival had been well publicised and hundreds of folk including the author of this book witnessed the event. It was reported that the crew took 15 hours to haul in the catch and at the much reduced speed of 2 knots, it took 22 hours steaming to reach port. The drifter/trawler LT215 *Lord Hood* was built by Cochrane & Son at Selby in 1925 for the Lowestoft Steam Herring Drifters Co. Ltd. and gained the port letters and fishing number of LT20 in 1949 after a period in Polish ownership. She saw service as a minesweeper in World War Two having been requisitioned in late 1939. At the time of winning the competition her owners were Pegasus Trawling Co. Ltd., a subsidiary of the Boston Deep Sea Fishing & Ice Co. Ltd. (*MWC*)

The 1953 Winning Drifter

PD417 Fruitful Bough - 323½ crans

This fine motor drifter was built in 1948 at the George Forbes Ltd. shipyard in Peterhead, the same yard that was responsible for building *Star of Bethlehem*, the 1951 competition winner. The winning catch, the largest ever landed during the Prunier Trophy competition, was made by *Fruitful Bough* about 25 miles from Yarmouth. Hauling in the nets went on from the evening of the 20th October until the afternoon of the 21st and lasted about 15 hours. The total number of herring caught and landed at Yarmouth was 419,000 when calculated at an average of 1300 herrings per cran. It was often the case that when a drifter's nets contained a very large amount of fish, some of the nets were transferred to another drifter because of the quantity and weight of the fish. Whilst the *Fruitful Bough* did not pass any nets to another drifter, during the competition YH29 *Ocean Lifebuoy* did pass nets containing around 63 crans to BF531 *Utopia* and yet still landed 301¼ crans at Yarmouth. Had she not handed over the nets to the Scottish drifter, the *Ocean Lifebuoy* would have easily won the Prunier Trophy that year. By the end of November most of the Scottish drifters had departed for home from Yarmouth and Lowestoft, much of the fishing by then being in the south on the Cap Gris Nez grounds.

Whilst returning home from Yarmouth after the 1961 season, *Fruitful Bough* ran aground a few miles north of Aberdeen in appalling weather. Thankfully the crew were unharmed, but the drifter became a total loss. *(MWC)*

The 1954 Winning Drifter

LK509 Jessie Sinclair - 272 crans

Built in 1945 as MFV 1166 at the yard of Walter Reekie at Anstruthur, *Jessie Sinclair* was one of the large number of wooden hulled motor vessels (MFVs) constructed to an Admiralty standard design during the Second World War. Many surplus MFVs were acquired by Scottish owners, several to replace ageing steam drifters. *Jessie Sinclair* was purchased from the Admiralty in 1948, her main engine being the usual four cylinder 160hp Lister Blackstone diesel installed in these craft. Under Skipper Robert Williamson she made her winning catch whilst fishing about 6 miles from Smith's Knoll, her crew taking approximately 7½ hours to haul in the fleet of nets before the drifter headed for Lowestoft where on 12th October, the opening day of the competition, she landed the record catch. Due to bad weather, the 1954 herring fishery was not one of the better seasons with gales and heavy weather seriously affecting landings and for the owners and crews causing damage to nets and gear. When the weather allowed, the drifters did land some very good catches in early October, examples being LT228 *Pecheur* with 226 crans, YH91 *Pre-Eminent* with 240 crans, and PD420 *Juneve* with 230 crans. Early November saw more good catches being made including Charles Eastick's KY322 *Wilson Line* that landed 270 crans at Yarmouth on 8th November, but later that month bad weather played havoc with fishing and landings became very erratic. The *Jessie Sinclair* was the only Shetland drifter ever to win the Prunier Trophy and many Shetlanders considered she should have been preserved. By 1954, the decline in the number of steam drifters, both English and Scottish, was becoming noticeable. Whilst a few left for new ownership, amongst those drifters sold for scrapping in 1954 from Lowestoft were *Acceptable, Buckler, Calm Waters, Flora Taylor, Herring Searcher* and *Patria*, while at Yarmouth twelve drifters were sold for scrap including the well known *Ocean Crest* and *Our Kate*. The name of *Ocean Crest* was soon reused at Yarmouth on a new vessel. (*MWC*)

The 1955 Winning Drifter

PD234 Morning Star - 210¾ crans

Caught at the time of the full moon, the *Morning Star,* arrived at Yarmouth with her winning catch on 1st November. The drifter, under Skipper George Duncan, had been fishing 35 miles north east of Yarmouth and it took the crew 12 hours to haul in the fleet of nets. Built at Thomas Summers shipyard at Fraserburgh in 1952, *Morning Star* passed to new owners in the early 1960s when her Peterhead port letters and fishing number were replaced by FR286. For 1955, the Prunier Herring Trophy competition ran from 11th October until 19th November. During October the drifters were fishing the Humber, Sole Pits and Smith's Knoll grounds but generally catches were well down on the previous year. Dense fog on some days and gales on many others, restricted fishing and the increasing numbers of large powerful foreign trawlers were blamed for the poor landings being made at Yarmouth and Lowestoft. No restrictions were placed upon the activities of these trawlers whose catching capacity was greater than that of even the largest drifters. The best landing made during October was that by the Silver Fishing Co. steam drifter LT46 *Silver Crest* when she landed 208½ crans at Lowestoft on the 31st, the day before the *Morning Star* landed the winning catch at Yarmouth. For the rest of November, few drifters made notable catches, the one exception perhaps being the 1919 built standard steam drifter YH47 *Ocean Dawn*, owned by Bloomfields Ltd., when she landed 140 crans on the 14th. After the disposal of several English steam drifters the previous year, many were surprised to see YH33 *Noontide* arrive at Yarmouth in the spring of 1955. Built at the Colby Bros., yard at Oulton Broad in 1918 and equipped with Crabtree machinery built in Yarmouth, she was previously Kirkcaldy registered. In the ownership of W. and L. Balls Ltd., *Noontide* was a very welcome addition to the diminishing numbers of English drifters, and in particular those Yarmouth based. The last steam drifter ever to be registered at Yarmouth, she was sold for scrapping in Scotland in April 1960. *(MWC)*

The 1956 Winning Drifters

FR156 Stephens - 215 crans

The 1956 competition ran from 9th October until 19th November and the result was unusual in that there were two winning drifters each landing 215 crans, one at Yarmouth and the other at Lowestoft. With a very poor 1955 season, many in the trade hoped that the fishing in 1956 would show an improvement. Unfortunately, the reverse happened and the herring landings for 1956 proved to be worse than those in 1955. This itself was substantially down on the amount of fish landed during the 1954 season. With no prospect of making good money and debts rising, in 1956 Scottish drifters started to go home in the middle of November. One of the few early highlights of the competition was the arrival at Yarmouth of LT246 *Fellowship* with 179 crans on 13th October. This diesel-powered drifter was converted from steam to diesel the previous year and before conversion, had been the steam drifter LT246 *Neves*. During a period of erratic and generally poor catches, on 20th October a few good landings were made by FR125 *Dayspring* with 212¾ crans, FR337 *Golden Harvest* with 207¾ crans, FR291 *Gleaner* with 201 crans and *Stephens* with 215 crans. This last landing was to turn out to be one of the two winning catches in the competition for 1956. As often happened on the fishing grounds, the *Stephens* had handed over nets containing about 40 crans to another drifter. *Stephens* was built as Admiralty MFV*1188* in 1945 by J. & G. Forbes & Co. at Sandhaven and fitted with a 160hp four cylinder Lister Blackstone diesel engine. The MFV was sold for use as a fishing vessel in 1947 and became FR156 *Wests,* in 1954 she was sold on and renamed *Stephens.* By the early 1980s, *Stephens* had been renamed *Poseidon* after passing into the ownership of Anne M. Elder of Gairloch. (*MWC*)

The 1956 Winning Drifters

LT46 Silver Crest - 215 crans

The steam drifter *Silver Crest* was built as the motor drifter LT381 *Larus* at the Cochrane shipyard in Selby at 1928. Following the rather unsatisfactory performance of her 210bhp 3 cylinder Plenty vertical internal combustion engine, her owner, the Alexander Fishing Co. Ltd. decided in 1929 to replace the motor with a steam engine. After being fitted with a 43nhp Elliott & Garrood triple expansion engine and Elliott & Garrood boiler, she was given a new fishing number and name and became LT46 *Silver Crest.* Following the conversion and change of identity, the drifter's owner was given as Mr. Arthur George Catchpole and partners. In 1940, the *Silver Crest* was transferred into the ownership of Silver Fishing Co. (Lowestoft) Ltd., and remained in that ownership until 1960, when she was sold for scrapping and left Lowestoft for a breakers yard in Belgium. *Silver Crest,* which was the previous year's runner up, tied with the Fraserburgh drifter *Stephens* for the trophy when she landed 215 crans at Lowestoft. Her winning catch was made just 16 miles north east of Lowestoft and landed at her home port on 22nd October. One aspect of the 1956 season was the noticeable decrease in the number of Scottish drifters participating in the fishery. Many of those that came south returned home early and others had not come south to Yarmouth and Lowestoft at all. The smaller number of drifters participating in the fishery due to poor catches and the economics of fishing were reflected in the amount of fish available on the markets and tended to make prices paid for the herring higher than in previous seasons. In the trade, the main reasons for the declining number of Scottish drifters were thought to be the more profitable fishing available around the Scottish coasts, consistent bad weather in the southern North Sea, but more importantly, the greatly increased trawling for herring by foreign trawlers on the traditional fishing grounds cleaning out the shoals. *(JWC)*

The 1957 Winning Drifter

KY124 Silver Chord - 212⅓ crans

An almost new drifter, being first registered in March 1957, *Silver Chord* was built by Alexander Aitken at Anstruther. She became the first and only Kirkcaldy drifter to win the Prunier Trophy when on 15th November she landed her winning catch at Yarmouth. Fishing 58 miles south east of the Corton Light Vessel, the crew took around 14 hours to haul in the nets, although some were lost and sank due to the weight of fish in them. At auction the herring made around £950. A change of ownership in 1975 saw the port letters and fishing number of *Silver Chord* change from KY124 to PD187. The 1957 season was considered fair by the trade with a slight improvement in the total amount of fish landed when compared with the previous poor herring seasons. With a decline in the number of drifters taking part in the fishery, those that did participate had slightly better financial returns due to more favourable market conditions. October saw many landings of over 100 crans at both Yarmouth and Lowestoft, examples of these being YH78 *Rosebay* with 175 crans of fresh and 25 of iced, LT279 *Quiet Waters* with 145 crans of fresh herring, and PD420 *Juneve* with 172 crans of fresh herring. After gales in early November, good catches continued with many of over 100 crans being landed by both English and Scottish drifters. However on 14th November, 45 Scottish drifters left Yarmouth for home, having decided that the best of the fishing was over. The competition ran from 8th October until 23rd November with many drifters working the Sole Pits in October and the traditional Smith's Knoll grounds in November. A change in the rules of the competition meant that the 1957 herring season would be the last when there was an official runner up. Two large drifter/trawlers came into the Yarmouth registry in 1957 when the Polish built YH370 *Autumn Sun* and YH372 *Autumn Star* arrived at the port. The addition of these two vessels and other new drifter/trawlers was welcome, but little compensation for the dozens of Yarmouth and Lowestoft vessels that had been disposed of in the previous ten years. (*MWC*)

The 1958 Winning Drifter

LT156 St. Luke - 162¾ crans

The drifter/trawler *St. Luke* was built at the shipyard of Henry Scarr at Hessle in 1950 and was one of five similar vessels that joined the Lowestoft fleet in the early 1950s, the others destined to spend most of their lives trawling. Fishing 12 miles north east of Smith's Knoll, the *St. Luke* made her winning catch on 24th October under Skipper Ernest Thompson, the skipper in 1952 of the steam drifter *Lord Hood* when she also won the Trophy. Skipper Thompson was the only skipper to win the competition twice. *St. Luke* was owned by St. Andrew's Steam Fishing Co. Ltd., a subsidiary of the Boston Deep Sea Fisheries Group, and was sold in 1961 to buyers in Chittagong, Pakistan. The 1958 herring season was considered a depressing affair, with few spectacular catches being made during the competition period and in late October, after the full moon, some of the Scottish drifters were preparing to go home. Because of the poor fishing and with no prospects of any great improvement, by the end of the first week of November, only 37 Scottish drifters were left fishing from Yarmouth. Ironically, the few good catches of the 1958 fishery were made after the Scottish drifters had all departed for home. However these were made on the Sandettie grounds near the Dover Straits and not the local grounds. (*MWC*)

The 1959 Winning Drifter

LT367 Dauntless Star - 189½ crans

This drifter/trawler was the second of two sisterships built in 1948 by Cochrane & Sons Ltd., at Selby. The first, LT371 *Dauntless Star,* was the winner of the 1948 competition. The winner of the 1959 competition, LT367 *Dauntless Star*, had a remarkable fishing career before winning the Prunier Trophy. Having originally been LT377 *Sunlit Waters,* she had a change of identity when she was renamed *Boston Swift*. In 1954 she crossed the Atlantic Ocean and fished Canadian waters as *Halifax No. 11*, the drifter/trawler then returned to Britain and worked out of Aberdeen as A143 *Swiftburn*. In 1958, she returned to her original home port of Lowestoft where she became LT367 *Dauntless Star.* The 1959 season was as depressing as the previous with few notable landings being made. The herring did not appear in any great quantities on the traditional Smith's Knoll grounds, and those that did were very patchy, with some drifters getting reasonable catches, whilst others fishing close by, caught only a few crans. The majority of the best landings came from other grounds, such as Silver Pits, much further away from Yarmouth and Lowestoft. Some drifters returned to port with very few herring or no herring on board to show for their efforts and late October saw the first Scottish drifters leave for home. The winning catch was made by *Dauntless Star* on 20th October about 40 miles north east of the Haisbro' Light Vessel. In 1968, her fishing days were over and after a period working as an offshore support vessel, in 1975 *Dauntless Star* left British waters again and headed for Dubai after being sold. (*MWC*)

The 1960 Winning Drifter

FR178 Silver Harvest - 187 crans

In 1960, it was the turn of a Scottish vessel to win the Competition when the Fraserburgh drifter *Silver Harvest* landed 187 crans at Yarmouth on 17th November. Caught about 48 miles south east of the Corton Light Vessel, the crew took around 16 hours to haul in the fleet of nets containing the catch which made over £1530 at auction. The Prunier Trophy competition ran from 11th October until 19th November but the herring were slow to appear on the traditional fishing grounds and it was late October before any good catches were made in the Smith's Knoll area. Early October saw drifters working the Sole Pits grounds with inconsistent results; many of the herring landed from there were iced or overdays, several drifters staying out longer than normal in the hope of finding the shoals. The landings during mid October were influenced by gales and industrial action by Scottish fishermen, but towards the end of that month and into November, landings did improve with a number of notable catches being made, including BF103 *Convallaria* with 151¼ crans and LT387 *Young Duke* with 168 crans, both of which sold for over £1200. The very last day of the competition saw LT173 *Boston Hornet* landing 154 crans at Lowestoft and PD326 *Fertile Vale* landing 120 crans at Yarmouth. The 1960 winner of the Trophy was built as MFV1049 for the Admiralty at the shipyard of John Morris (Gosport) Ltd., at Fareham in 1945. She was sold out of naval service and converted for fishing in 1947 when she became FR178 *Silver Harvest*. In the mid 1960s, she was sold to Irish owners and was given the port letters and fishing number of D171, but retained her original name of *Silver Harvest*. In the early 1980s, she was still recorded as fishing with that identity. *(MWC)*

The 1961 Winning Drifter

LT61 Dick Whittington - 274½ crans

Built at the Lowestoft shipyard of Richards for Small & Co. (Lowestoft) Ltd., the drifter/trawler *Dick Whittington* was launched in January 1955 and ran sea trials during the following March. She was one of two similar vessels built by Richards that year for Small & Co., the other being the LT137 *Norfolk Yeoman*. Early October found some drifters working north of Smith's Knoll on the Indefatigable Banks, although good catches were made there, the quality was poor and the prices paid at auction reflected this. Bad weather kept drifters in port during mid October, but when they could get to sea and start fishing, good catches were made in the Smith's Knoll area, examples being the 196½ crans landed at Yarmouth by FR87 *Xmas Star* and the 170 crans landed by KY322 *Wilson Line*. The winning catch of the season was landed at Lowestoft on 23rd October by the *Dick Whittington*, the crew, under Skipper Leo Borrett having spent 15 hours hauling in the nets containing an estimated 370,000 herring. Other notable catches around this time included FR329 *Radiant Way* with 180 crans and FR346 *Tea Rose* with 145 crans, both of which were landed at Yarmouth. With a few exceptions, from the end of October and throughout November catches declined with gales and generally poor fishing causing problems for the skippers. By mid November the fishing had moved south to the Sandettie grounds, where a few good catches were made, but by then the majority of the Scottish drifters had gone or were preparing to go leaving around 45 at Yarmouth and none at Lowestoft. By the third week in November, skippers were trying their luck further south on the Cap Griz Nez grounds off the French coast, where FR249 *Excelsior* made a reasonable catch of 77 crans, which she took for auction at Lowestoft. *Dick Whittington* was sold in 1968 to new owners in Trapani, Sicily where she was renamed *Saturno II*. (*MWC*)

The 1962 Winning Drifter

YH61 Ocean Starlight - 294⅓ crans

The attractive colour scheme adopted for the steam and diesel powered vessels of the Bloomfield fleet was a much admired feature of the British herring industry for many years. Drifters belonging to this much respected Yarmouth owner had the misfortune to miss winning the Prunier Trophy on a number of occasions, often landing large catches before the start of the competition or after it had finished. Skipper Stanley Hewitt was the first Bloomfield skipper to win the competition, when in 1962, he brought the *Ocean Starlight* into Yarmouth on 9th November and landed the winning catch that had been caught 40 miles north east of Smith's Knoll. During early October, drifters were making reasonable catches on the Dowsing grounds and by the third week in October, herring were to be found on the fringe of the Smith's Knoll grounds. As had happened during previous seasons, the shoals were getting smaller and it was becoming very difficult to predict where they would be, one drifter could get a very large amount of fish whilst another, fishing a short distance away, would only get a few crans. Some drifters were fishing over 90 miles from port in an attempt to locate the elusive shoals of herring. In addition to a decrease in the number of English drifters taking part in the fishery, fewer Scottish drifters were participating with a combined total of 63 vessels compared with a total of 96 the previous year. *Ocean Starlight* was one of a pair built at the Lowestoft shipyard of Richards Ironworks in 1952 and was first registered on 3rd October 1952. She was sold to Lowestoft owners in 1963 and given the new port letters and fishing number LT465. In September 1967, *Ocean Starlight* was sold on to Dutch buyers, but returned to East Anglian ownership in 1972 and was converted for offshore support work. This once well known drifter/trawler was later sold to Milford Haven owners as the standby safety vessel *Dawn Spray,* and was scrapped in 1995. (*MWC*)

The 1963 Winning Drifter

LT137 Norfolk Yeoman -186½ crans

The sistership to the Prunier Trophy winner of 1961, the *Norfolk Yeoman* was launched at Richards Ironworks in 1955 and became one of the fine fleet of drifters and trawlers operated by Small & Co. (Lowestoft) Ltd. and their many subsidiaries. By 1963, the industry was well accustomed to poor herring seasons, but was ever hopeful that the once vast shoals would reappear with heavy landings of good quality fish again seen on the markets at Yarmouth and Lowestoft. The competition period for 1963 was from 7th October until 23rd November and the first good landing during that period was by LT467 *Ocean Surf* when she put ashore 120 crans at Lowestoft on 16th October. *Ocean Surf* was one of the six Yarmouth drifter/trawlers previously owned by Bloomfields Ltd., at Yarmouth that had been purchased in 1963 by Small & Co. (Lowestoft) Ltd., and given new Lowestoft port letters and fishing numbers. Due to poor fishing, some Scottish drifters headed for home in October but as had happened in the past, the end of November saw a substantial upturn in the fishing, with large catches being made by the Lowestoft and remaining Scottish drifters, particularly in the area to the south east of Smith's Knoll and about 80 miles from Yarmouth. However, the shoals appeared very patchy with evidence of this being provided by FR305 *Fertile*. Fishing 70 miles south east of Yarmouth, she caught an estimated 700 herring overnight and her skipper, Andrew Tait, decided to stay out and try again the next night when an estimated 407,000 herring were caught. The winning catch made by *Norfolk Yeoman* under Skipper Ritson Sims on the Hinder fishing grounds, was landed at Lowestoft on 7th November; some of the herring were already boxed whilst the rest were still in the nets. The *Norfolk Yeoman* was sold in 1968 with the *Dick Whittington,* and the two left Lowestoft on 14th June with *Norfolk Yeoman* carrying the name *Eros I. (MWC)*

The 1964 Winning Drifter

LT671 Suffolk Warrior - 276½ crans

A superb product of Richards shipyard at Lowestoft in 1960 and the last of the type to be built there, the drifter/trawler *Suffolk Warrior* was also one of the last two of that type built for English owners, the other being the *Boston Hornet.* The competition ran from 6th October until 28th November, but gales in early October resulted in little fishing activity and it was not until the second week in October that any worthwhile catches were landed. The majority of landings were well under 100 crans with some as small as a few boxes to show for a nights fishing. During the third week in October landings did improve, with a number of Lowestoft drifters including *Dauntless Star, Young Elizabeth, Harold Cartwright* and *Ethel Mary* all making landings of between 150 and 200 crans at Lowestoft. Yarmouth landings were made by Lowestoft drifters *Young Elizabeth* on 24th October and *Ethel Mary* on the 24th. During this run of good fishing, Skipper Ernest Fiske took the *Suffolk Warrior* into Yarmouth with the winning catch of the season. Fishing 20 miles north east of the Smith's Knoll light vessel, the crew had taken some eleven hours to haul in the catch. The erratic landings and general poor fishing of early October returned as November approached, resulting in some of the Scottish drifters going home. As had happened in the past, the last half of November saw an upturn in the fishing for a brief period, with some drifters landing good catches including that of FR34 *Star of Hope* when she put ashore 189 crans at Yarmouth on 21st November. The *Suffolk Warrior* was lost on 15th February 1969 in the North Sea following a collision with the Dutch trawler *Hendrike Johanna;* the crew were safely picked up by the Dutch trawler. (*LESMS*)

The 1966 Winning Drifter

FR346 Tea Rose - $128\frac{2}{3}$ crans

With no claims being submitted during the 1965 season, it was decided by the Herring Industry Board that the Prunier Herring Trophy would not be awarded that year. The 1965 season was described by those in the trade as "dismal", "depressing" and "pathetic". Hopes were that the 1966 season might show an improvement. Early landings in September from the Silver Pits area were reasonable, but the fishing in October started slowly with few good catches being made and the majority of the herring landed were small and of poor quality. A spread of good landings later in October was mixed with depressing catches for others. Some of the Scottish drifters made reasonable landings during this time, examples being FR305 *Fertile* with 100 crans, and FR487 *Sunbeam* and PD72 *Venture* with 125 crans each. The end of October saw some of the Scottish vessels still doing well and it was during this time, on 25th October, that *Tea Rose* landed her winning catch at Yarmouth. The landings of the Lowestoft drifters in general were poor and perhaps justified the few local vessels participating in the fishery. By early November many of the Scottish drifters, including *Tea Rose*, were back in Scotland having left Yarmouth before the competition ended. At Yarmouth in 1966 the number of Scottish drifters was around 30, whereas in the early years of the competition this figure was over 400. During the 1930s, the total number of English drifters working from Yarmouth and Lowestoft was around 300. The total number of English drifters participating in the 1966 fishery was six, five Small & Co. vessels plus Mr. James J. Colby's drifter LT382 *Wisemans*. FR346 *Tea Rose* was ordered by the Admiralty as MFV1217 and completed in 1946 at the Fraserburgh shipyard of Wilson, Noble and Co. as a fishing vessel. FR346 *Tea Rose* was her third identity; earlier in life she had been LK367 *Mary Watt* and FR346 *Branch*. As already mentioned, the 1966 Prunier Herring Trophy competition was the last ever. *(MWC)*

The Colour Images

A once familiar autumn herring season scene on the East Anglian coast as a steam drifter leaves one of the herring ports for the fishing grounds and meets a north easterly gale full on. (*MWC*)

BK235 *Fleetwing*. Built in 1903 at Eyemouth.
At Yarmouth, November 1938 (*MWC*)

INS39 *West Neuk*. Built in 1910 at Selby.
At Yarmouth, November 1938 (*MWC*)

BCK440 *Available*. Built in 1912 at Selby.
At Yarmouth, November 1938 (*MWC*)

WK12 *Sweet Pea*. Built in 1912 at Lowestoft.
At Yarmouth, November 1938 (*MWC*)

The scene at Lowestoft in the Waveney Dock in 1930, with many drifters present and no apparent spare space in the dock. The drifter in the centre with the crew checking the nets is PD185 *Craigentinny*, built in 1919 at Northwich and owned by A. Strachan and partners of Peterhead. (*LESMS*)

In the adjacent Hamilton Dock, drifters take up every available space on the quayside. The nearest drifter, LT227 *Reclaim,* was lost in November 1937 with nine of her crew following a collision off Lowestoft. The stern of LT757 *Regain* can be seen behind the *Reclaim*, she was lost in August 1939, also following a collision. (*LESMS*)

For over fifty years during the herring season at Great Yarmouth, drifters and swills dominated the harbour area during this period of great activity. These scenes were recorded in October 1938 with many drifters, almost all Scottish, landing their catches.

Above Left-From left to right, vessels that can be identified are: BCK3 *Loranthus*, BCK209 *Jeannie McIntosh*, FR221 *Star of Light*, KY175 *Copious* and YH81 *Craiglea*. *(MWC)*

Above Right-From left to right, vessels that can be identified are: PD266 *Monarda*, BCK433 *Coreopsis*, FR269 *Dewy Rose*. *(MWC)*

Yarmouth in the early 1950s with the steam drifter PD382 *Rossard* on the left and the motor drifter FR531 *Xmas Rose* on the right. In the centre with the green hull and red funnel is YH73 *Rose Hilda*. (*MWC*)

Another Yarmouth Fishwharf scene from the same period showing an Eastick owned drifter and another drifter alongside. Herring is being swung ashore in a quarter cran basket that is then emptied into a swill. (*MWC*)

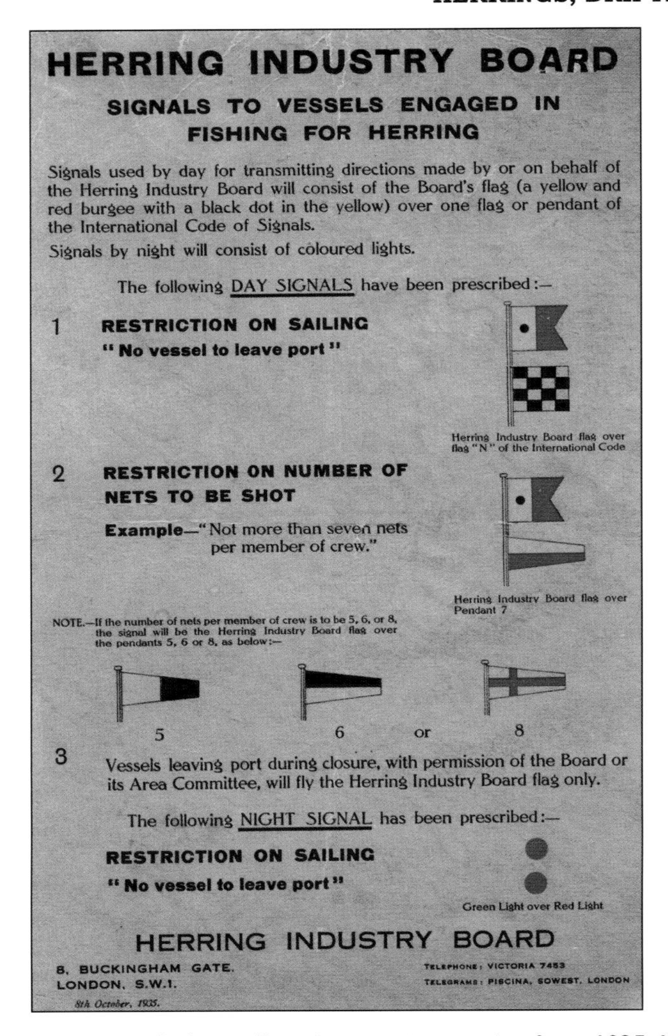

HERRING INDUSTRY BOARD

SIGNALS TO VESSELS ENGAGED IN FISHING FOR HERRING

Signals used by day for transmitting directions made by or on behalf of the Herring Industry Board will consist of the Board's flag (a yellow and red burgee with a black dot in the yellow) over one flag or pendant of the International Code of Signals.

Signals by night will consist of coloured lights.

The following DAY SIGNALS have been prescribed:—

1 **RESTRICTION ON SAILING**
" No vessel to leave port "

Herring Industry Board flag over flag "N" of the International Code

2 **RESTRICTION ON NUMBER OF NETS TO BE SHOT**
Example—"Not more than seven nets per member of crew."

Herring Industry Board flag over Pendant 7

NOTE.—If the number of nets per member of crew is to be 5, 6, or 8, the signal will be the Herring Industry Board flag over the pendants 5, 6 or 8, as below:—

5 6 or 8

3 Vessels leaving port during closure, with permission of the Board or its Area Committee, will fly the Herring Industry Board flag only.

The following NIGHT SIGNAL has been prescribed:—

RESTRICTION ON SAILING
" No vessel to leave port "

Green Light over Red Light

HERRING INDUSTRY BOARD

8, BUCKINGHAM GATE.
LONDON, S.W.1.

TELEPHONE: VICTORIA 7453
TELEGRAMS: PISCINA, SOWEST, LONDON

8th October, 1935.

A rare Herring Industry Board restrictions notice from 1935. In order to accommodate the notice in this book, it has been reduced in size. An example of the flag signals in use can be found on Page One. (*MWC*)

A Scotch fisher girl tops up a barrel of herring with brine on a pickling plot at Sandringham Road, in the Roman Hill area of Lowestoft and well away from the docks. A bung can be seen on top of the nearest barrel, to use for plugging the hole after completion of the topping up.
Pickling plots were spread over a large area in Yarmouth, Gorleston and Lowestoft with many being located in the back streets. (*LESMS*)

The Scottish drifter PD214 *Utilise* at Yarmouth during the herring fishing of 1967. At the time she was owned by members of the Duthie family of Peterhead. With no English drifters operating from Yarmouth in 1967, it was the Scottish drifters plus a few visits by Lowestoft drifters that maintained Yarmouth as a fishing port. *(SJ)*

During the herring fishing, many townsfolk at Yarmouth and Lowestoft visited where drifters were discharging their catches in the hope that herrings had dropped out of the basket or trunk being swung between the vessel and the quay. It was normal practice for passers by to "acquire" free of charge, any fish that had dropped on the ground. Several herrings are seen here awaiting to be "collected" at Lowestoft in this scene from 1956. The general use of the aluminium trunks seen on the right started in the 1950s and these replaced baskets, and the wooden boxes which were of a similar size and shape, some of which can be seen beyond the aluminium trunks. Despite the initial outlay in buying the trunks, they were far superior in many ways to baskets and wooden boxes. *(Studio 161)*

As mentioned elsewhere, a large open area on the Denes at Lowestoft was used for drying nets and this view from the early 1930s shows part of that area. Most of the buildings in the background were associated with the fishing industry, some being net stores and beating chambers. *(LESMS)*

Another rare 1930s colour image, this time of Scottish steam and motor drifters moored on the north wall of the Hamilton Dock at Lowestoft. One Lowestoft drifter, LT476 *The Boys,* is on the left. *(LESMS)*

The wooden steam drifter YH530 *Queen of the Fleet* was launched on 5th May 1917 at Richards shipyard in Lowestoft, with her first owner, Mr. C. A. Webster, paying £1750 for the hull. Later in life she was owned by members of the Woodhouse family of Winterton and eventually passed into the ownership of members of the George family, also of Winterton. The *Queen of the Fleet* had a 39nhp Burrell engine and a boiler made by Riley Brothers of Stockton-on-Tees. She is seen here leaving Yarmouth for the fishing grounds and passing an inbound Peter-head steam drifter. *Queen of the Fleet* was sold for breaking up in 1947. (*MWC*)

A fine early colour image showing Scotch girls topping up barrels with salted herring ready for the lid to be put on, and for the topping up with brine to be carried. (*LESMS*)

Just before the bung is put in the barrel by the chap in the back ground, the barrel is topped up with brine by the Scotch lass. (*LESMS*)

The Yarmouth steam drifter YH105 *Wydale* left her home port on 29th October 1961 bound for a breakers yard in Holland. She was the last steam drifter to operate from a United Kingdom port. These views of *Wydale*, still with her Prunier Trophy winners weather vane on her mizzen mast, are from a series recorded at Yarmouth three weeks before she set off for Holland. Further information about this typical wooden Lowestoft built steam drifter can be found on Page 80. (*DW*)

Two of the three active smoke houses in Lowestoft, The Old Smoke House and Anchor Fisheries, are situated adjacent to the A12 London-Great Yarmouth trunk road and are seen by thousands of travellers every day. These are the buildings of Anchor Fisheries, in Katwijk Way. The other, that belonging to fish merchants J. T. Cole, is situated in what was once the beach village, and only a short distance from the sea wall. It is easy to find since the tallest wind turbine in Britain is located close by. (*MWC*)

One English drifter and many Scottish drifters share this view of the Hamilton Dock at Lowestoft. The English vessel, YH105 *Wydale* is on the extreme left, and has possibly landed her catch at Lowestoft where prices were higher than at her home port of Yarmouth. (*Studio 161*)

A superb view of LT224 *Justifier* entering the Waveney Dock at Lowestoft in 1956. In addition to many diesel powered drifters belonging to Small & Co. and their subsidiaries, several other well known English drifters are also to be seen including *Welcome Home, Coastbreeze, Impregnable, Lord Hood, Lord Keith, Shepherd Lad* and *Primevere*. During the 1950s, the Scottish drifters were usually accommodated in the Hamilton Dock. The *Justifer* was built in 1925 at Selby and was owned by E. T. Capps & Sons Ltd. She was sold for scrapping in January 1958 to Belgium . During the Second World War, *Justifier* was assigned the pennant number FY736 and served as a minesweeper. *(Studio 161)*

The drifter/trawler LT343 *Madame Prunier* was originally the Scottish owned PD388 *Equity I*. She *was* built at the Brooke Marine shipyard at Oulton Broad in 1948 and is seen here at Lowestoft in 1956. (*Studio 161*)

Many English drifters including YH167 *Ocean Sunlight* share the north wall of the Waveney Dock at Lowestoft with Scottish drifters. The 1952 Prunier Trophy, LT20 *Lord Hood*, has just arrived from the fishing grounds and makes her way towards the quay in a space between LT181 *Lord Keith* and LT1118 *Impregnable*. (*Studio 161*)

A peaceful scene at Yarmouth in the mid 1950s with Scottish drifters at rest near the Town Hall. Those drifters that are identifiable are PD110 *Honey Bee*, FR359 *Sunrise* and PD297 *Fairweather*. (*MWC*)

Another group of smart Scottish drifters seen on the same day, but further along the quay. On the left is FR371 *Brighter Hope* owned by the Caledonian Fish Selling & Marine Store Co. Ltd. (*MWC*)

A Selection of English, Welsh and Irish Registered Drifters at Lowestoft, Yarmouth and Southwold

LT505 *Esther* at Southwold. Built in 1877 at Southwold. (*MWC*)

YH378 *Primula* off Yarmouth. Built in 1893 at Yarmouth. (*MWC*)

LT595 *Sweet Promise* at Lowestoft. Built in 1893 at Porthleven (*MWC*)

YH707 *Fortunatus* entering Yarmouth. Built in 1902 at Lowestoft (*MWC*)

YH797 *Boy George* entering Yarmouth. Built in 1903 at Yarmouth. *(MWC)*

YH485 *HFE* entering Yarmouth. Built in 1909 at Lowestoft. *(MWC)*

LT531 *Girl Ivy* at Lowestoft. Built in 1902 at Lowestoft. *(MWC)*

LT180 *Playmates* leaving Lowestoft. Built in 1925 at Selby. Lost with all hands in March 1955 *(MWC)*

The drifter/trawler LT770 *Beacon Star* in the Waveney Dock at Lowestoft. Built in 1911 by Cochrane at Selby, *Beacon Star* was reported missing with her crew of nine in February 1937. She is believed to have been lost in bad weather in the area near the Eddystone Lighthouse (*MWC*)

SN83 *Quintia* leaving Yarmouth. Built in 1914 at Yarmouth.
(*MWC*)

SH47 *Girl Annie* entering Lowestoft. Built in 1910 at Lowestoft.
(*PKC*)

WY187 *Jesburn* entering Lowestoft. Built in 1917 at Oulton Broad.
(*MWC*)

LY921 *Carrigart* entering Lowestoft. Built in 1912 at Inverness.
(*MWC*)

YH202 *Comely Bank* entering Yarmouth. Built in 1914 at Portgordon. (*MWC*)

YH29 *Ocean Lifebuoy* entering Yarmouth. Built in 1929 at Aberdeen. (*MWC*)

M72 *Val* entering Lowestoft. Built in 1909 at Grimsby. (*PKC*)

HL88 *Clara Sutton* leaving Lowestoft. Built in 1917 at Oulton Broad. (*MWC*)

YH138 *Animation* leaving Yarmouth. Built in 1925 at Lowestoft. *(MWC)*

YH972 *Bulrush* leaving Yarmouth. Built in 1907 at North Shields. *(MWC)*

YH217 *Frons Olivae* leaving Yarmouth. Built in 1912 at Yarmouth. Lost after striking a mine on 12th October 1915. *(MWC)*

LT495 *Thistle* approaching Lowestoft. Built in 1904 at Lowestoft. *(MWC)*

The wooden steam drifter LT375 *Welcome Friend* was built in 1914 at Oulton Broad by Colby Bros. with machinery being supplied by Elliott & Garrood. She was owned by Gilbert & Co. who sold her for breaking up in Holland in July 1939. (*MWC*)

YH296 *Ocean Hunter* at Yarmouth. Built in 1919 at Oulton Broad. (*MWC*)

LT345 *Primevere* at sea. Built in 1914 at Aberdeen. (*MWC*)

LT750 *Golden Miller* leaving Lowestoft. Built in 1910 at Selby. (*MWC*)

YH92 *Achievable* at Lowestoft. Built in 1927 at Oulton Broad. Entering Lowestoft dry dock (*MWC*)

YH55 *Young Ernie* leaving Yarmouth. Built in 1924 at Lowestoft. (*MWC*)

YH225 *Fortitude* leaving Lowestoft. Built in 1945 at Grimsby. (*MWC*)

LO488 *Susan M* entering Lowestoft. Built in 1945 at Lymington. Lost with all crew in November 1957, believed destroyed by a mine. (*MWC*)

PZ85 *Karenza* at Lowestoft. Built in 1942 at Whitstable. (*MWC*)

LT318 *Friendly Star* approaching Lowestoft. Built in 1946 at Plymouth. *(JWC)*

LT90 *Dawn Waters* leaving Lowestoft. Built in 1930 at Yarmouth. Originally steam powered *(MWC)*

YH377 *Ocean Trust* approaching Lowestoft. Built in 1957 at Lowestoft *(JWC)*

YH370 *Autumn Sun* at Yarmouth. Built in 1956 at Gdansk. *(MWC)*

The Yarmouth steam drifter *Girl Nancy* was followed by the diesel powered *Ocean Sunlight* in being assigned the port letters and fishing number YH167. **Top**-*Girl Nancy* at Yarmouth with members of the crew on deck. Built in 1910 by John Chambers at Lowestoft, after having a number of local owners she was sold in 1934 to a lady in Essex. and converted into a steam yacht. In 1987, her remains could be seen on Bridgemarsh Island in Essex. (*MWC*) **Bottom**-A much later vessel, the drifter/trawler *Ocean Sunlight* was built at Lowestoft by Richards in 1952. After many years of good fishing for her owners, Bloomfields Ltd., she was sold to Lowestoft owners in 1963. *Ocean Sunlight* was sold by them to Dutch buyers in 1967 and as the *Orion*, was lost with all hands later that year. She is seen here at Lowestoft leaving on a Sunday morning with Lowestoft drifters for the fishing grounds. (*JWC*)

Built in 1930 at Yarmouth by Fellows & Co. as Yard No. 325, YH73 *Rose Hilda* was sold in 1954 to Lowestoft owners and became LT90 *Rose Hilda.* She was converted to diesel propulsion and renamed *Dawn Waters* (See page 121). *Dawn Waters* eventually passed into Milford Haven ownership, and her fishing registry was given up in December 1974, the vessel having been scrapped. (*MWC*)

A view of the river at Yarmouth in the mid 1950s from the lantern platform of a lightship.
The following drifters can be seen laid up and with a doubtful future:- YH92 *Achievable,* YH471 *Ocean Swell,* YH578 *Phyllis Mary* and the second vessel to have the identity of YH217 *Frons Olivae.* It is not possible to identify the remains of a wooden steam drifter just beyond the other drifters. (*MWC*)

Built in 1960 at Brightlingsea, the drifter/trawler LT173 *Boston Hornet* is seen here in use as an offshore support vessel. Entering service when drift net fishing was coming to an end, the opportunity to earn good money on work other than fishing, was eagerly taken up by many owners. (*MWC*)